SENIOR SERVICES FOR THE FINANCIALLY CHALLENGED

NAVIGATING MEDICAID SERVICES, ASSISTED LIVING FACILITY PLACEMENT AND SO MUCH MORE

By
Davida Siwisa James

i

ISBN-13:   978-1984100979
ISBN-10:   1984100971

A society that doesn't treasure the knowledge, experience and wisdom of the elders is in trouble.

Dr. David Suzuki

Warning Label

The information I share in this book was prompted by my personal experiences in caring for my elderly father who had dementia and then Alzheimer's. A woman I know who spent decades in the senior care community said, "I didn't know that" so many times at information that I was discovering that she finally said, "You really should put all that information in a book."

At the writing of this, my dad is 93 and still kicking.

This information is meant to help well-intended, caring people with limited funds who want to help themselves, their elderly parents and / or loved ones live with a modicum of dignity. The book is "not" designed to assist dishonest, abusive or manipulative people outwit the system or in any way take advantage of seniors. Though I am powerless to stop that, I needed to write this caveat and discourage such actions. Meaning – don't take advantage of people, especially seniors and the disabled. Please. Not good. Bad Karma. Do unto others... What goes around comes around, etc.

ALSO, I am not a lawyer, mental health professional, or social worker. Nor am I an elder care professional. Again, this is written based on my experiences, my opinions and the personal research I have done gathering information over the course of seven years. So if you think it wise, take what I've written with a grain of salt... or a hillside of salt. Double check my assertions and do your own research as well!

There is a certain part of all of us that lives outside of time. Perhaps we become aware of our age only at exceptional moments and most of the time we are ageless.

Milan Kundera

TABLE OF CONTENTS

DEDICATION

THANK YOU to all caregivers the world over who truly do provide loving, selfless care to those who no longer have the physical or mental capacity to care properly for themselves. You perform a daunting and often thankless job. I applaud you answering the call to do this important work for families…for our society.

… and

To my father, David "Turk" McNeil: ours was not a conventional father/daughter relationship, whatever that may mean. And in the end, you had one more life lesson to teach me: how to care for an aging parent.

What mothers need, as well as fathers, spouses, and the children of aging parents, is an entire national infrastructure of care, every bit as important as the physical infrastructure of roads, bridges, tunnels, broadband, parks and public works.

Anne-Marie Slaughter

FORWARD

Before my 87-year old father moved in with me, I barely
understood the difference between Medicare and Medicaid. For
simplicity, I will use the term "Medicaid" but in California this
government program is called "Medi-Cal." I knew absolutely
nothing about senior support services, except that Meals on
Wheels delivered something akin to TV dinners to the elderly. I
never had to buy a porta potty for the home, Ensure, other
nutritional supplement drinks or adult diapers. In this journey of
caring for my father, which was far from a happy time in my
life, I learned so many things the long, hard way.

It was a tedious, upsetting, frustrating, surprising and unpleasant
experience – both the hunt for clear information and taking care
of Dad. Trying to gather material to help him and having people
give you confusing or conflicting information was one of the
worst parts.

That frustration and the angst I went through caring for my
father is the primary reason I wanted to write this book. First, I
really wanted to try to provide some good basic information to
spare you – my fellow caregivers who are financially challenged
– from some of what I went through over six years of gathering
vital data. I remember once calling that senior service
connection that is advertised on TV and radio all the time, "A
Place for Mom and Dad." The first thing I learned was that
everything they deal with is private pay. They don't handle
Medicaid placement. And while I have no doubt this is a
wonderful resource for people who have ample resources and
are seeking long-term care placement, when you don't have
much money it is a short conversation. When I called, the

questions on the other end quickly evolved to what the family could contribute to my dad's limited financial resources. So I knew right away that I needed to keep doing research. This book is the result of that and is intended to help families that have very limited resources. But some of the information will be beneficial to you no matter what your income.

My second reason for writing this is to say, "It's OK to be miserable and frustrated. It's OK to not enjoy taking care of an elderly person, even if it is your spouse, mom or dad. It doesn't make you a bad person." That doesn't mean you shouldn't undertake to be as patient and compassionate as possible. But it is not going to be fun a lot of the time. It is stressful. I was depressed for 95% of the five years that my dad lived with me. And forgive me every time I say 'I' or "me" because Dad lived with my husband and me. And without my husband, I could not have managed.

Here's the thing: too many people want to guilt you into feeling like you are a bad person if you don't feel all warm and fuzzy about taking care of someone who is wetting the bed, crapping on themselves, leaving poop on the toilet seat, asking you the same question five times in ten minutes, and generally not aging gracefully. They want you to tell them what a blessing it all is.

And you know what? For the people who have had a warm and fuzzy, loving relationship with their parents (and assume I also mean spouses, partners and significant others) and they feel like emptying their urine and wiping their butt is an honor, I admire you greatly. I applaud that kind of dedication and unselfish blind loyalty and love. I mean that. I am not being sarcastic. You are saintly. But for the rest of us realists, it can be depressing and really unpleasant.

Not all spouses had a great relationship during their time living together that would make them want to administer this level of care in old age – despite the "for better or worse" part of the vows. Not all children had a loving close relationship with their parents. My own father left me alone to fend for myself in New York City when I was 17. Yet I found myself having him under my roof in his old age much longer than I was ever under his roof as a minor.

Different agencies and medical professionals all but threatened to report me for neglect for wanting to give up Dad's care to a facility or the state. I jokingly asked a sheriff once if I could report Dad for having abandoned me as a teenager. I was 63 at the time I posed the question. The sheriff told me he was pretty sure the statute of limitations had passed. He smiled when he said it.

And, yep, I get it. There's a chance I might be in that situation one day – needing someone to care for me – and so might you. If so, I pray to God that it's a nurse OR "caring" senior attendant changing my diapers and not my husband or son. I took my son to lunch on his 36th birthday, when my dad was still living with us, and I gave my child a note. It basically read, "If I ever get to the point in my old age where I need professional care and it is beyond you, you have my absolute blessing to put me in a home. And you are going to want to hold on to this note because you might have to show it to me one day." I told him that I never wanted to be the cause of him and his wife arguing over my care or me negatively impacting their marriage by living with them.

And so to the purpose of this little book: I am writing it because of all those people who were constantly shocked by me telling them about things I had discovered that they didn't know about. And that shocked me. Because what does it say about the system if you are talking to a person who works in the senior care services field, and they don't know about some of the services available?

Much of this information is also applicable to services for the disabled. But I have no experience in researching that field and no personal experience with it. You would need to verify what information transfers to a disabled person in your care.

The last thing is that some services will apply to any senior and some specifically to those who have not yet moved into dementia. You might have free or reduced-fee public transportation available to seniors, but clearly you are not going to send someone with advanced dementia out on a bus alone and just cross your fingers that they get back home.

And this is not intended to be a comprehensive guide to senior services. There are a lot more things available of which I have no personal experience. While I did some extra research in the writing of this book to try to be thorough, most of this involves what I went through in caring for my dad.

So…here goes: chapter and verse, hopefully told with a tad of humor and a lot of honesty, with a few anecdotes in between about the good, the bad and mostly the ugly bits of maneuvering your way through taking care of an elderly person, and senior care services when you are financially challenged.

I think you will find it helpful. I hope so.

THE DECISION TO BECOME A CAREGIVER and Caregiver Resources

The decision to bring an elderly parent or relative into your home to care for is a serious one. And it is not one that should be done out of high emotion, on a whim or for financial reasons. Bringing them into your home is the easy part. Moving them out of your home to a safe, clean place where they will be well cared for is a lot harder. It could take months or years and countless hours of research and phone calls.

If you are having financial difficulties, it might seem like killing two birds with one stone to bring the senior into your home. You provide your loved one with a safe caring place to live and also have them share in household expenses. I suggest you make sure you are totally ethical in this path because there are strict elder laws that could see you on the other end of an abuse claim if you misuse their funds. Plus, it's just not right.

You might find yourself rethinking the decision to bring a senior into your home once they get to the stage where they are leaving the gas on, or the bathroom door open, forgetting to put on pants, or you are a prisoner in your own home because they can't be safely left alone. That's why if you do decide to become a caregiver, you need to make yourself aware of all the various support services that can help you cope.

Knowing what I do now, I would have left my father in his lovely studio apartment in the senior building in which he was living in Philadelphia. It would have been better to work to get him more Senior In-Home Support Services at his apartment, rather than paying a small fortune to move him across country to live with us in California. My husband and I had only lived in our home (our first home purchase) for 18 months when we moved Dad in with us. That's all. And suddenly our new home had to be adapted for my father and his truck full of belongings.

That is another thing to consider – the physical space. You may have to do some juggling to accommodate the senior. There are practicalities to sharing your home, and some of it could entail some selfish feelings with having to rearrange your home. Be prepared for that. And, again, it doesn't make you a bad person.

Also, there is a reason they say, "Pride goeth before a fall" [Or... more precisely "Pride goeth before destruction and a haughty spirit before a fall." Proverbs.] Many seniors refuse to admit they need help and refuse to accept their frailties. At 93, barely able to walk, with dementia and incontinence my father still questions why he needs to be in an assisted living facility, preferring that my husband and I play attendant to him. Whereas my Aunt Margaret used to joke about the fact that she was wearing diapers, and had a portable toilet in her bedroom. She accepted her "new normal" and made the best of it with humor and grace.

Seniors, especially those with dementia, can get downright nasty about any suggestion that they are not the same alert person they once were, that their home is not as clean, that their wardrobe choices are not as well put together, that the smoke alarm is going off because they keep burning their food, that ten minutes is too long to heat food in the microwave, that they are confused about medications or that they are having "bathroom incidents" that are affecting their personal hygiene and your sanity. As a matter of fact, increased aggressive responses are one of the symptoms of dementia.

My dad used to be something akin to a Playboy in his prime in Harlem. He dated a tall, gorgeous, curvy Cuban Radio City Music Hall Rockette (photo below). Carmen was also in the original Broadway production of "West Side Story." Beautiful women flocked to him. He was a bartender who knew legendary Jazz musicians who would sit on the bar stool and shoot the breeze with him. He was self-taught, with very little formal education, a man who had subscriptions to The New Yorker, The Smithsonian, Life, Look, Playboy, and season theater tickets. He donated to public television from back in the 1960s, and he cooked gourmet meals that would have rivaled those of top chefs. He was going on Scandinavian cruises in the 1960s, long before black folks knew much about cruising, and in the days when people dressed formally for dinner. My dad was a cool guy, and he dressed like someone who had their clothes tailor made. He was the epitome of suave. That was David "Turk" McNeil.

Dad and Carmen, circa 1960, his Latin girlfriend who was in the original Broadway version of "West Side Story." She had also been a Rockette.

Yet by the time he came to live with us when he was 87, something much bigger than a 180 degree change had occurred. The first thing that struck me was that he was sometimes willing to go out in public in outfits that at one time he would not have worn alone in his home. And then the next day Dad would get dressed up like he was about to have a photo shoot with GQ Magazine. Pointing out the crazy dress days to him wound up causing arguments. Getting him to put on a jacket when it was 40 degrees outside was a debate over why he needed more clothing.

Discovering that the unpleasant smell I was noticing was from pants that had been urinated in and hung back up in the closet, shocked the hell out of me. This man who used to marinate a Leg of Lamb for two days in his own concoction of sauces and a half dozen herbs could no longer fry an egg.

My father had dementia, developed Alzheimer's and progressively got worse. He refused to believe that he was having accidents and peeing in his pants, even if you gave them to him as evidence. Everything I have described was his worsening condition. He called us liars for saying he had left the bathroom in deplorable conditions that I won't detail or that he had asked us the same question 52 times in a row.

I learned early on, in an Alzheimer's support group, that you are not supposed to ever say, "You just asked me that OR don't you remember I told you so and so." That only angers the person with dementia and sounds like you are rubbing it in that their memory is failing. But here's the thing: we are all human. And patience is a virtue that I didn't always exhibit. When Dad would ask me the same question four times in a row, I would try to answer as if I was hearing the question for the first time. But by the fifth time, I was done. My answers then were exactly what you were not supposed to do. This is how the conversation would go:

- Dad, you asked me that several times and I told you we are going to L.A. tomorrow.
- I didn't ask you before. If I knew that, I wouldn't have asked.
- But you did ask. You asked four times.
- Well, you don't have to rub it in. You don't have to make me feel bad that my memory isn't what it used to be.
- But here's the thing, Dad: I don't get credit for having answered you four times already without saying, "I told you that." I only get grief from you because I was fed up by the fifth time. So I can't win. You don't know it was the fifth time.
- =pause= Is that happening to me? Did I really ask you five times? What's happening to me?

At which point you feel like crap because you see what your loved one is going through. Suddenly, you feel like a jerk for being annoyed enough to say, "You asked me that."

Yet not every senior gets dementia or Alzheimer's, thank God. Not everyone with mild dementia progresses to Alzheimer's. There are a million scenarios. By now, it's common knowledge that Alzheimer's can develop absent the person ever having had the milder stage of dementia first.

There are plenty of seniors who age gracefully and are still driving, doing Yoga, golfing or swimming, traveling, helping with the grandkids, living on their own, making their own decisions, having love affairs, taking French lessons, cooking their own omelets and living productive healthy lives well into their 80s and 90s. That's the blessing. That's what we all pray our "golden years" will be like.

I didn't realize what I was getting myself into when I invited Dad to come live in our home. And I began to regret it from day one.

One should think very carefully about the decision to become a caregiver to the elderly because there is a lot involved. Eventually, if their dementia or physical condition worsens you could become the cook, dishwasher, laundress, chauffeur, cleaning lady, secretary, business manager, shrink and nurse. You are in for an endless parade of forms and applications to keep up with getting the senior all the services they need. Medicaid? Great, but you have to continue doing the annual recertification process (unless the senior is getting SSI as well).

A lot of people don't have the temperament to provide this kind of care. That's where elder abuse comes in – people who are not suited for this level of care get stressed and lash out. Or… people suited to it get overwhelmed and lash out.

Despite the fact that Dad definitely contributed financially for rent, food and utilities, I didn't know for five years that there was a Department of Aging that would have paid for someone to help with some of the extra care that I was providing him. He was my father, and the thought hadn't crossed my mind.

After a while I started resenting that my life, my relationship with my husband, and my retirement had turned into being the nursemaid and caregiver to a man who had always put his own interests ahead of being a father. Despite the fact that I have always given my dad so much credit for exposing me to the finer things of life, to nurturing my love of theater and music, to allowing me to see a way out of the ghetto and being able to make better choices about the kind of person I wanted to be… we still had spent more years apart than under the same roof. He still had not 'raised' me in the more typical sense. He still left me to my own devices alone in New York City at far too young an age.

After Dad had complained for the tenth time in a few days about his condition, and asked if anything could be done I said, "Dad, you are 91-years old. Some people experienced what you are going through in their 70s. Sometimes you act like you never expected to get old."

His response: "Not this old."

I am blessed to have a husband who has a stronger sense of family than I ever did. I actually feel my dad prefers my husband – who he calls Wonderful Rob – more than me.

Once again, think carefully before you make the decision to become a caregiver. And establish a really good rapport with the senior's doctor. It will help you tremendously, as the doctor is your best advocate for many of the social services I detail.

Our society must make it right and possible for old people not to fear the young or be deserted by them, for the test of a civilization is in the way that it cares for its helpless members.

Pearl S. Buck

ORGANIZING YOURSELF

This may seem like a silly thing to put in a book, but it's important. Invest in a few file folders.

As you go through this journey, you will be inundated with letters, paperwork, research material, copies of packets of information you've filled out, and documents from lots of agencies.

The last week that my dad lived with us was very stressful. The social worker from the Hospice Agency asked for a copy of my Power of Attorney and Dad's latest medical directives. It took me about three minutes to return with both. He looked at me surprised and said, "I have seldom seen anyone this organized."

<u>Some folders you should set up:</u>

- Social Security / Medicare
-
- Medicaid // Medi-Cal
-
- Copies of I.D. and income statements
-
- Senior Services: like the Department of Aging
-
- Medical records: you should know the names of all doctors, specialists, have a list of medications, and any printouts showing diagnoses (especially of dementia and Alzheimer's)
-

- Legal Documents (Last Will and Testament, Medical Directive, Power of Attorney)
-
- Contact Information: make sure you have a list of friends and family who would want to know of any hospital admissions or death
-
- Life Insurance forms: You should know where the form is that allows you to designate the funeral home as the payee when your loved one dies (if this is appropriate), and all the current forms showing the beneficiaries.
-
- Funeral Home research: costs for regular funerals, as well as cremation

NOTES:

_____

_____

_____

LEGAL STEPS

Elder Law is an entire specialized area of the law that is designed to protect the rights of senior citizens. Make sure everything you do in caring for the senior and managing their affairs is done so legally, fairly and with good intentions. Many states have enacted laws to protect seniors. For instance, California has the Older Americans Act and Older Californians Act.

If you make the decision to bring a senior loved one into your home (or even if you live in their home), there are very important steps you may want to take so that you have the legal power to act on their behalf. Otherwise, you will not be able to get critical information from some of the agencies and medical professionals with which you are dealing. And some will simply not speak with you unless you put the senior on the phone. Usually, despite being my father's only child, the first question I would get was, "Do you have Power of Attorney" OR "Are you their designated medical directive appointee?"

One would assume that between husband and wife or domestic partners that the other person is automatically in charge of the legal affairs for their better half. This may or may not be true, and it is impossible for me to guide you here because it probably varies by state. So these are suggestions that could help everyone.

But for adult children caring for their parents, there is definitely no 'given' that because your parent is living in your home that you have the legal right to make decisions for them. This book is meant to help those of us who find ourselves caring for parents who can no longer afford where they were living because of limited funds, or whose physical and/or mental conditions preclude them from living alone anymore. Most of the time, either we are moving in with them or they are moving in with us. And, of course, it could be that they are still living at home, and you are coordinating services to keep them safe and healthy.

Consider the following:

- Conservatorship: A conservatorship is where a judge appoints a responsible person or organization to care for an adult who cannot care for themselves or manage their own finances.
-
- Documents: Once you accept this responsibility, you should be as organized with your senior's important papers as you are with your own. Make sure you create a file or envelope with:

  - Lease or deed to property, banking info
  - Important phone numbers for people who need to be contacted in case of emergency
  - Copies of I.D. and/or originals
  - Financial documents / records
  - Medical Records
-
- Power of Attorney: This gives you the legal right to handle their affairs. Do this while the senior is still sane, lucid, clear thinking and can make decisions so no one can accuse you of manipulating them while they were not in their right mind.

- Medical Directive: If appropriate, make sure you (and possibly another person to share this responsibility) have the power to make medical decisions. This can be through the Physician's Order for Life Sustaining Treatment (POLST) or other advanced medical directive forms (like California's FIVE WISHES).

-

- Last Will and Testament. Unless you are a blood relative or 'extremely' close to the senior, don't guide them through this alone or hold all this powerful information for yourself. Make sure someone else is aware that the senior has made a Will and where these documents are located. I've prepared Wills for a couple of people and then they took it to a Notary. Many people feel you have to have a lawyer to make out a Will. Not true, especially when you are talking about people who generally don't own more than the possessions in their home. And I doubt the courts will be getting involved with a low-income senior with little money. But it could avoid family squabbles if there is some indication of what the senior wanted in terms of disbursing their personal belongings. Legally, anyone can simply write down their wishes and have it witnessed (preferably by a third party who is not getting a bequest). There are countless online examples of wills and very inexpensive "kits" that you can get online that will guide you through this process. Then just pay a notary $20 or so to validate the signatures.

-

- Lease and/or Deed: Every situation is unique. If this is a close loving relationship, and depending on other family dynamics, protect your rights as well. If you have given up your own living space to go live with the senior, make sure you won't be out on the street the day after they pass away. Perhaps you can be added to the lease as a tenant or have some ability to stay in the home for a certain period of time. Discuss this with the senior, other family members, and perhaps a housing rights advocate. I'd suggest writing up some kind of agreement that at least gives you six months or so to find alternative living arrangements.

▪
▪ <u>Life Insurance:</u> Beyond a certain age, most seniors can only get a small burial policy – maybe $1,000-$5,000. It will vary by insurance company. Whatever it is, make sure you get the necessary form ahead of time from the insurance company so when the time comes you can sign it over when dealing with the funeral home. There is a specific form for this. There may be other funds available to handle funeral expenses. But if not, you want to have this form at hand. A lot of people don't realize that the large policy they paid into for decades ends at about age 85.
  o <u>Term:</u> pays a death policy to beneficiaries during a specified term.
  o <u>Whole Life:</u> This type of policy builds cash value that can be deducted from periodically (borrowed from) or adds to the final death benefit.

Think of other legal and business matters specific to your senior. You may have V.A. benefit forms or other important documents you want to make sure you can access.

MEDICARE, MEDICAID

and

THE MEDICAID ASSISTED LIVING WAIVER PROGRAM

You are never too old to set another goal or to dream a new dream.

Les Brown

THE DIFFERENCE BETWEEN MEDICARE and MEDICAID (and the ASSISTED LIVING WAIVER PROGRAM – ALW)

www.medicare.gov/

MEDICARE is the federal government medical plan that everyone who has worked throughout their lives gets at AGE 65 after they have contributed enough money into the system to qualify for this. It is that ultimate end of the rainbow plan that you pay taxes into all your life. It goes hand-in-hand with Social Security. If you've paid enough taxes to get Social Security, you've also paid enough to get MEDICARE.

I was indignant when I got my first Social Security / Medicare statement when I was in my early forties. Most of us think of these plans as something for old people. And at 42, I did not want to feel like an old person eligible for Social Security or Medicare. I actually called the Social Security Office, indignant, and asked them why they were sending me statements already. The woman I spoke to said, "Miss, you should be very happy. That means if you never work another day in your life, you've paid enough into the system that you will collect Social Security and get Medicare." That shut me up.

What happens if you are still working and have other medical insurance or you are on your company's retirement health plan when you turn 65? Medicare begins to pick up the insurance payments that your company once paid. So let's say right before you turn 65 you were covered under Cigna or Blue Cross on your company's plan. You paid the employee portion and the company paid the bulk of the premium. At age 65, your portion of the payment ends and so will the company's portion. You could switch over to "Cigna or Blue Cross" as a senior advantage program through Medicare. In some company retirement plans (like the University of California system) you might actually get paid a small bonus for now being on Medicare to help you pay your Part B premium.

You are required to register or apply for Medicare when you approach 65; generally, you should apply three months before your 65th birthday. If you started collecting Social Security early, you will automatically be enrolled in Medicare.

If you earn over a certain amount of money through your own income or retirement (approximately $925), you will be required to pay your portion of the Medicare Part B premium. That could be at least $105 a month or so. But if you do qualify for Medicaid, this monthly premium for Part B can often be paid for by Medicaid.

MEDICARE (Parts A, B, C and D)
- Part A is your hospital benefit.
- Medicare Part B covers doctor's visits and some medical equipment. There is a premium for Part B.
- Part C are the health plans offered by private companies that contract with Medicare *to provide you with all your Part A and Part B benefits.* Medicare Advantage Plans include HMOs (like Kaiser Senior Advantage or Blue Cross). Usually these plans also provide your medications.
- Part D is for prescription drug coverage.

Not everything is covered by "straight" Medicare (Parts A & B); hence, most people have additional supplemental plans in which they enroll to help 'augment' or add to their Medicare benefits (Part C plans). You may recall seeing these commercials on TV frequently where different medical plans are trying to convince you to sign up for their plan to augment your Medicare coverage.

Medicare is not something you get because you are low-income (that is Medicaid). Yet you could easily have worked all your life and still have a low enough income at retirement that qualifies you for Medicare and Medicaid. You get Medicare because you worked and paid taxes.

MEDICAID (called Medi-Cal in California - same thing)
www.medicaid.gov/
Link for state-by-state summary of benefits:
https://www.medicaid.gov/medicaid/by-state/by-state.html

Medicaid is a federally funded medical plan, financed by 'federally subsidized grants' directed to each state. Many states supplement the Medicaid fund with additional state funds. EACH state has its own eligibility requirements and other regulations.

Medicaid eligibility is based on both your monthly income AND assets (or resources). Generally, as long as your home is your primary residence, you can still own a home and get Medicaid assuming there are circumstances that have now reduced your income to the Medicaid eligibility standard. Check your state's regulations.

Medicaid is intended to provide medical services to "low-income and disabled" individuals who do not have the means to have their own private-pay medical plans. The emphasis here is on low-income. An individual or couple can't earn $40,000 a year and receive Medicaid, even if you don't have your own insurance. In that case, you need to find your own medical plan, be added to a spouse or domestic partner's plan, look into government-subsidized plans or pay out of pocket.

I believe this is what happened with the Affordable Care Act (commonly known as Obama-care). A lot more folks with very low incomes started applying for Medicaid. I am only familiar with eligibility for seniors.

Many people have Medicare AND Medicaid. If the senior has a low enough income – earned and/or Social Security payment ($925 or less... but check that figure), they may be eligible for both. IT IS ADVISABLE that you have the senior apply for Medicaid if their low income warrants it. There are a host of services and co-pay subsidies that Medicaid helps with above and beyond for which Medicare pays. For instance, the senior goes to the doctor for an X-Ray and there is a $50 co-pay. If they are on Medicaid, this is paid for and not out of pocket for the senior.

BUT remember that if you are married your joint income is considered for Medicaid eligibility. And while married people may have low enough income individually to get Medicaid, their joint income may disqualify them.

Medicaid enrollment also helps to pay for your Medicare Part B premium. For anyone who does not require the full Medicaid services, you can apply for the QMB portion, which just pays the Medicare Part B premium.

Key Facts: Income Definitions for Marketplace and Medicaid Coverage

http://www.healthreformbeyondthebasics.org/key-facts-income-definitions-for-marketplace-and-medicaid-coverage/

Each state has different income limit requirements, though I doubt there are huge differences. That's probably because Medicaid is a joint federal-state program. The following is based on California regulations. Your household income is based on your family's size and can't exceed 138% of the federal poverty level.

CALIFORNIA ANNUAL INCOME LIMITATIONS:
One person: $16,395
Two people: $22,108
Three: $27,821
Four: $33,534
Five: $39,248

These income limits are based on a family's Adjusted Gross Income, which is the sum of an individual's gross income (total earnings subject to income tax) minus deductions for certain expenses. By my understanding this is NOT the same as income minus the standard IRS tax deduction. I advise you to double check this. But the amounts above will clearly let you know that you can't be a single person earning $40,000 a year and be eligible for Medicaid.

NEW YORK STATE MEDICAID INCOME LIMITS
(seniors, disabled and blind)

Income	**$842** (up from $825 in 2017)	**$1,233** (up from $1,209 in 2017)
Resources*	**$15,150** (up from $14,850 in 2017)	**$22,200** (up from $21,750 in 2017

*Resources
Resources (aka "assets") are money and property owned by an applicant for public benefits. Different programs have different rules about what types of resources are counted towards the resource limit, and some programs have no resource limit at all. In general, resources include bank accounts, other financial institution accounts, and real property **(except the primary residence).**

http://www.wnylc.com/health/entry/15/

MEDICAID ASSISTED LIVING WAIVER PROGRAM [ALW] or [ALP]

NATIONWIDE ASSISTED LIVING FACILITY DIRECTORY
https://www.assistedlivingfacilities.org/directory

Every state has an Assisted Living Waiver Program (ALW) or (ALP) that is subsidized by Medicaid. I will refer to this as **ALW**. These "grants" or "subsidy" programs are set up to help low-income people who qualify for Medicaid pay for the greater part of the costs for enrollment in an Assisted Living Facility. You must research the requirements and coverage area for your state and county, as there will be variations to program requirements.

Assisted Living means that the senior needs help with some important life function: e.g., bathing, bed mobility, dressing, eating, toilet use or administering medications. This is not the same as skilled nursing, where the staff are medical professionals.

There is a broad range in terms of the accommodations and quality of the facility. There are very high end facilities that look like a classy hotel or resort. There are others that may make you cringe. In some facilities, the senior could have their own studio or one-bedroom apartment with a private bath where they can move in with their own furnishings. Most do not have kitchen facilities but might have a mini fridge and/or microwave. Others might be a shared room with twin beds and a shared bathroom and may or may not have a fridge and/or microwave.

But this program is a very well-kept secret that is entirely public if you just do the research. The link I provided above gives you access to information on assisted living facilities nationwide.

Within the state page, you should find the guidelines for that state's ALW program, as well as other valuable details about senior services and the Department of Aging Services.

Medicaid Share of Cost: For most of these ALW programs, the senior needs to be fully on Medicaid with no SHARE OF COST. This is important because there are some people whose income or assets require them to have a 'Share of Costs." That means if an individual enrolled in Medicaid has income or assets that exceed the limits for regular **Medicaid,** a certain amount of monthly medical bills will need to be incurred each month before **Medicaid** is approved. This is your **"share** of **cost**." You will need to check with your county/state with an ALW program to determine whether your Share of Cost means you would be disqualified for the ALW program or if it just means your share of the monthly payment to the Assisted Living Facility would be more than the person who is on regular Medicaid with no share of cost.

This is an important distinction, as someone once entered the wrong code for my father while he was on the program. We were then notified that his portion of the monthly rent to the facility was going to increase significantly.

I found out about the ALW program through sheer frustration. There is a very high-end Assisted Living Facility in the Mojave High Desert where I was living called Sterling Commons. This is one of those $5,000 a month places and it looks like a four-star hotel. I went there to interview one of the residents when I was a freelance journalist for the local newspaper. Later, I complained to a colleague of mine that it was a pity that when you are poor you have no access to the nicer facilities like

Sterling Commons and could wind up in a dump where you have to worry whether your loved one is being neglected. This woman was a regional manager for the Alzheimer's Association in Southern California, and she commiserated with me over the lack of services for low-income seniors. So she had no clue either.

I was increasingly frustrated over the place that looked like the Hilton and some of the ones that wind up being featured on a 60 Minutes-type exposé on abuse in care facilities. It prompted me to email Dad's social worker for his medical plan. I asked her whether there was any help available for people on Medi-Cal to get a break with long-term facility care costs.

To my utter shock, she told me about the Medi-Cal Assisted Living Waiver Program. I kept asking, "What do you mean?" because I couldn't believe it. Eventually, after many steps and mis-steps I got Dad's application started, got him admitted to a five-star facility for about a year, then because of a lack of communication lost the waiver. Then he got re-enrolled in an odd way that I describe in the section titled SSI.
Each state and county's program can vary in terms of:
- the amount of funds dedicated for this program
- whether all the spaces are filled for the program
- if your state's Medicaid program is no longer taking applicants
- whether there is a waiting list to get a waiver
- how the condition of the senior is ranked (the more able bodied are given less priority)
- That there are a limited number of Assisted Living Facilities that accept the Medicaid Waiver.
- That not every facility accepts them, so you have to find one… and one that has an opening

But there is no question that a lot of Medicaid recipients have no idea that this program even exists. Even people who are very familiar with the state and county public welfare benefits are often surprised to hear of this program.

I told that colleague of mine who worked for the Alzheimer's Association about the ALW program, and she was stunned. Since then, I have spoken to many professionals in the health care and senior services field who were just as surprised. Many of them started scribbling notes when I told them that I had my father enrolled in an excellent assisted living home under the California Medi-Cal Assisted Living Waiver Program.

This is 'verbatim' what is written in a flyer that I was given by a "major" HMO in Southern California:

> The cost of such care at an RCFE (Residential Care Facility for the Elderly) is paid for at the individuals' or families own expense. Care provided at an RCFE does not qualify to be paid for by Medicare, your health insurance company, or Medi-Cal.

Wrong! So wrong. This flies totally in the face of the fact that every state has a MEDICAID ASSISTED LIVING WAIVER PROGRAM to help Medicaid recipients pay for this care. So if a major HMO is giving out erroneous information (quite innocently I am sure), that speaks to why I wanted to compile the information in this book.

Also, there are long-term care insurance plans that are very costly, but can help pay for at least some period of time in an Assisted Living or Skilled Nursing Facility.

The ALW program is not necessarily everywhere:
Sometimes states will only have this program available in certain counties. In some states, you might encounter a waiting list that could take months before you get assigned a waiver. I was also told by a nurse who did the assessments for the program that there are times that patients in a skilled nursing home will receive priority to get approved for the ALW before a senior already living in the family home. I think the logic here, as I was told, is that the person who already has a home may not be seen as needing to be placed as much as someone who is in a skilled nursing facility and needs to transfer to an assisted living facility. Of course, that doesn't take into account the anxiety family members may be enduring in terms of their personal desire to get their loved one placed in a facility.

Some states, like Georgia, have their own state-subsidized program in addition to or in combination with the Medicaid program. And I am sure that from state to state, you might find shorter or longer waiting lists or more availability with these waiver programs.

THESE ARE THE STEPS YOU NEED TO BE PREPARED FOR IN APPLYING FOR THE ALW and SNIPPETS OF SOME OF THE FORMS:

The Facility:
This could be the same in most states, but as you apply for the ALW in California they prefer to know that you have a facility lined up that has an opening and an ALW bed. When we toured the five-star facility in Riverside where we placed Dad the first time, they actually gave us the entire packet of forms to be completed and a referral to the nursing agency that could do the needs assessment.

Some care facilities are exclusively Medicaid patients. The greater majority are private pay, and they reserve a certain portion of the rooms, suites or beds in a shared room for the ALW. But in the time that it takes for you to get approved by Medicaid, the bed could be assigned to someone else. That means you need to try to have at least two or three facilities lined up that have an opening or keep checking availability as the application is being processed. Assuming you are approved for the program, you will have a multitude of additional forms to fill out upon admission to the facility.

And while my focus was on an assisted living facility, board and care facilities may also take the ALW. You will need to check when you call the various facilities.

The major resource to find a residential care facility that will take your senior is probably the listing on your state's website for the agency that licenses these facilities. In California, this agency is the California Department of Social Services - Community Care Licensing that licenses these care facilities. Most people will want to know the facility has a state license.

In California, go to:
www.ccld.ca.gov

-Click "Find Licensed Care" on the RIGHT side of the page in a little square.

-Most likely you will want to click on "elder assisted living"

-You will be taken to a page that asks you to sort by facility type, city or county

From the list that pops up, you can click on a specific facility. From there, you can begin to build a list based on your criteria. Most people want a facility that is not too far from the family in terms of visiting the senior. You must then do your due diligence in terms of calling to get information, viewing their website and making a site visit. Get the names of everyone you speak with and the date in case you are given erroneous information. Ask if they have an opening and if they accept the Medicaid Waiver. If you establish a good rapport with them, an administrator may call you back if a bed or apartment opens up. It is best to have more than one facility that you know has a vacancy.

Always ask if the facility has a certain amount of beds reserved for Social Security residents. This is basically a "charitable" situation where a facility is willing to accept just what the senior gets in Social Security. In larger residential care facilities, they may have enough room to save a few beds in this category.

The Doctor:
A doctor must be on board with the senior's need for care in an assisted living facility because the following form (which is three or four pages) will need to be completed and signed by the doctor. So discuss this carefully with the doctor beforehand. No matter what you may think, if the doctor's notes here do not support someone who requires extra care for "assistance with living," that's pretty much the end of the road. You don't want to get the form signed too soon as you will also be required to provide a negative TB skin test or chest X-ray showing there is no active TB. And this can't be more than a year old.

Be aware that there are certain medical conditions that could get the senior denied admission to a facility: Stage 3 or 4 pressure sores, being actively on chemotherapy, wound-vac therapy or an active infection. Either the facility or the nurse who does the needs assessment will advise you on this.

PHYSICIAN'S REPORT FOR RESIDENTIAL CARE FACILITIES FOR THE ELDERLY (RCFE)

I. FACILITY INFORMATION (To be completed by the licensee/designee)

1. NAME OF FACILITY   2. TELEPHONE

3. ADDRESS   CITY   ZIP CODE

4. LICENSEE'S NAME   5. TELEPHONE   6. FACILITY LICENSE NUMBER

II. RESIDENT/PATIENT INFORMATION (To be completed by the resident/resident's responsible person)

1. NAME   2. BIRTH DATE   3. AGE

III. AUTHORIZATION FOR RELEASE OF MEDICAL INFORMATION
(To be completed by resident/resident's legal representative)

I hereby authorize release of medical information in this report to the facility named above.

1. SIGNATURE OF RESIDENT AND/OR RESIDENT'S LEGAL REPRESENTATIVE

3. DATE

The medication profile is quite simple and just lists all medications.

MEDICATION PROFILE

Page ___ of ___

❑ NKA ❑ Allergies, Reactions, Sensitivities
Pharmacy   Phone
Infusion/Enteral Company   Phone
Physician "A"   Physician "B"
Physician "C"   Physician "D"

MD Code	Date New	Date Changed	Date D/C	Medication/Strength	Dose	Freq	Route	Initiated Date	Initials

The Needs Assessment:

A nurse or social worker (usually through an agency) handles these assessments of the senior for the Medicaid ALW Program. It is to the agency that you will most likely submit the forms you have the doctor complete and they will forward to the Medicaid Office.

A nurse will come to your home to assess the senior to determine what level of care they require. Be nice to this person! Remember that it is their determination at this interview that decides whether the senior is eligible for residential care. This is a bit of a joint interview in that they will want to hear from you (the caregiver) in terms of what you do for the senior. Then they will look at the senior's room, bathroom and any other space that is dedicated to the senior's use. They will interview the senior separately as well.

Most care facilities contract with a particular local nursing agency to do this assessment. The level of care the senior requires provides the facility with needed information on how to care for the resident. It also determines how much money Medicaid pays to the facility – the greater the care the senior requires, the higher the payment to the facility.

After the assessment is done, the nurse will write up a report that is sent to the Medicaid Assisted Living Waiver Program with your other forms. If you do not automatically receive a copy of this report, you can request it. Along with other factors, this review of the senior's needs is what Medicaid uses to determine if the senior is eligible for the ALW program and at what level of care.

If someone is at a level 0 or 1, it might be questionable if they would be admitted to the program because they are still mostly self-sufficient. This is especially true if they are already residing in your home or their own home and looking to move to an Assisted Living Facility.

The report states the level of care by:
0= independent 1= supervision/overseeing 2=limited assistance
3= extensive assistance   4= total dependence

SCORING: 0 = Independent 1 = Supervision/Overseeing 2 = Limited Assistance 3 = Extensive Assistance 4 = Total Dependence						Score
BED MOBILITY – *(how client reposition self in bed)*	0	1	2	3	4	
TRANSFER – *(how client changes positions and transfers between surfaces)*	0	1	2	3	4	
LOCOMOTION IN RESIDENCE – *(how client moves around the residence)*	0	1	2	3	4	
DRESSING – *(clothing, braces, splints, prosthesis)*	0	1	2	3	4	
EATING – *(meal set-up, cuing and how client eats and drinks)*	0	1	2	3	4	
TOILET USE / INCONTINENT - *(ability to use toilet, or use of incontinence pads)*	0	1	2	3	4	
PERSONAL HYGIENE – *(how client maintains personal hygiene)*	0	1	2	3	4	
BATHING – *(how client takes bath / shower)*	0	1	2	3	4	
					Total Score:	

INCOME LIMITATIONS FOR ALW

If your income is a little too high, some states allow the senior to work out something to still qualify for help. But there are states that impose an "income cap," which means a potential resident won't be eligible for the ALW or Medicaid if the resident's income exceeds a certain amount, unless the excess income above this amount is paid into a special trust.

Sometimes referred to as **Qualified Income Trusts**, or **Miller Trusts** (based upon a court case with the same name), they are used when a Medicaid applicant has too much income to qualify for Medicaid but not enough to pay for nursing home care or other long-term care costs. The senior places the 'excess' income or assets in this Miller Trust and they or their spouse can draw small monthly payments from the Trust.

These issues are outside of my experience and something you would need to research more, consult Medicaid or an elder law attorney.

I realize this may sound somewhat contradictory since the base requirement for Medicaid is that your total monthly income is "really" low (like under $1,000 a month). Check on this particular "trust" requirement carefully.

There are also several books on the market that go into detail about how to protect your assets from nursing homes. Some of these are specific to a particular state. Below are a few, though I do not advocate either the process or one book over another. But if you do know that you are 'close' to being eligible for Medicaid and that you need to go the Medicaid route in terms of long term care, do the research necessary to figure out your financial status.

The Medicaid Planning Handbook: A Guide to Protecting Your Family's Assets from Catastrophic Nursing Home Costs
by Alexander A. Bove, Jr.

How to Protect Your Family's Assets from Devastating Nursing Home Costs: Medicaid Secrets
By K. Gabriel Heiser, Attorney

Medicaid and Nursing Home Costs: How to Keep Your Family Assets Protected   by Atlantic Publishing Group, Inc.

The income cap states as of this writing in 2018 are: Alabama, Alaska, Arizona, Arkansas, Colorado, Delaware, Florida,

Georgia, Idaho, Indiana, Iowa, Kentucky, Louisiana, Mississippi, Nevada, New Mexico, New Jersey, Oklahoma, Oregon, South Carolina, South Dakota, Tennessee, Texas, and Wyoming.

Again, not my area of expertise, so consult others for more precise information.

ASSUMING YOU ARE APPROVED FOR THE ALW:

Stay proactive in checking with the nursing agency that did the assessment and the facility as to the status of your application. The nursing agency will let the facility know that you have been approved (and they should apprise you). Once your ALW application is approved, you only have a limited amount of time to make sure you get your senior admitted to a facility. If you miss that deadline, you lose your space and would need to reapply. I believe you have three months, but verify this. Coordinate the move with the facility, as you will have admission forms that you need to complete with them as well. Once your senior is approved for the ALW program and you have scheduled the move-in date, you will also need to make arrangements for paying the senior's monthly share of the fee.

Most facilities will charge the senior as "rent" all but $150 or so of the senior's income. That means the senior gets to keep about $150. Medicaid will pay the balance of the facility fee. The quality of the facility is only limited by your research and which one accepts the waiver.

Again, there are five-star facilities that accept the ALW vouchers, and there are some of the shady ones and everything in between.

DON'T LOSE YOUR ALW VOUCHER!

If, for some reason, you move the senior out of a facility in which you have had them - based on the ALW - you must move them into <u>another</u> facility that accepts the voucher WITHIN 30 days… or you LOSE the voucher. That means that you would have to start the process all over in terms of the applications, doctor's visit and forms, assessment and waiting list. Depending on your state and the agency you are working with that assessed your loved one, you might have up to 60 days.

PLEASE read the above again.

No one told me this. I never got a letter from Medicaid, was never told this by any social worker, nurse or the first Assisted Living Facility in which I placed my dad. I moved him out because the facility was not a memory care facility and Dad's dementia got progressively worse. The facility had warned me that if his dementia got too bad I would need to remove him since they were an "open-door" facility. That means no buzzer to restrict access. Understandably, they did not want the liability for Dad wandering out.

My husband and I brought Dad back home with us. And when we realized just how much his condition had deteriorated, we immediately started looking for a facility that would take the ALW voucher, but specialized in Alzheimer's. There weren't a lot of them and many were full, but we found one. I was shocked when I discussed this with the nursing agency that had done Dad's assessment initially only to be told that because it was four months later that we had lost the voucher and would have to start from scratch and reapply. At that particular time, Medicaid had put a freeze on new applications in our county.

Don't lose your voucher! If you are going to take the senior out of one facility, make sure you have a new one lined up first that will accept the voucher and your loved one. And do it within 30 days!

SUPPLEMENTAL SECURITY INCOME (SSI) AS ANOTHER WAY FOR ADMISSION TO A RESIDENTIAL CARE FACILITY FOR THE ELDERLY (RCFE)

Assume these facts to be true.

- The senior is receiving a low enough amount on Social Security that they qualify for Medicaid.
- The senior is enrolled in Medicaid.
- The senior gets admitted to an Assisted Living Facility where you pay the full fee or an adjusted amount.
  THEN
- The senior can immediately apply for SSI, based on now ALREADY being in an Assisted Living Facility. The senior's income might have disqualified them for SSI before - but being admitted to the facility changes everything.

AND – assuming they are approved

- Medicaid will then pay the balance of the senior's fees for the Assisted Living Facility. So essentially, this is a different way to get into the Medicaid Assisted Living Waiver Program because the senior is already admitted to and living in a facility.

AND

- Once the senior is on SSI, they "automatically" qualify for Medicaid. So that means that you will no longer have to do the annual recertification that you normally do for a senior receiving Medicaid.

This is exactly what happened with my dad. We were blessed to find a facility (through the great help and contacts of a dear friend) that admitted my father to its Assisted Living Facility and accepted the very small amount of Social Security that Dad was receiving. When I admitted Dad, the administrator said, "You should go to the Social Security Office right away, take these admission papers and tell them that your dad is here now. They will give him an additional amount under SSI."

I didn't know what this 'extra' amount would be, only that it would be a little more than what Dad was currently receiving.

When I went to the Social Security office, the clerk explained the steps I described on the previous page. Obviously, nothing is guaranteed. You apply, submit all the

paperwork and the senior has to be approved for SSI. If all goes well, the senior will be approved for SSI, and receive a little more money.

Medicaid will then contact the facility to make arrangements to pay the balance of the facility fees for the senior.

We often hear about whether or not a certain famous person is 'aging gracefully' or 'aging well.' But that usually refers to their physical appearance. Have her eyelids dropped? Does he have a double chin? How much weight has she put on?

I have come to learn that this outward appearance is meaningless when it comes to aging. Body parts are going to change. Our minds are going to change. I would much rather have my slide into old age be one that is marked by continued kindness, a respect for others, an appreciation for the care they provide me, and an acceptance – with grace – that I am simply not the person I once was. I am an older me, a different me.

D.S. James

SOCIAL SECURITY AND BECOMING THE SENIOR'S PAYEE

Most of us know that Social Security payments are the primary retirement income for millions of seniors in the United States. Ideally, this is combined with savings, a retirement plan from your employer or your personal 401K retirement plan. But for millions of Americans, Social Security is their only source of income at retirement.

Anyone who calls Social Security an "entitlement program" is doing a disservice to all of us who work our whole lives contributing to this program. It's an entitlement program only in the sense that we've paid into this federal system through our taxes our entire working lives, and we are entitled to get this retirement benefit any time after age 62.

Checks sent directly to the senior's bank
Many years ago the government started insisting that all Social Security payments be made by direct deposit to the senior's bank. This may differ in some areas of the country, but is the general rule of thumb now. I grew up in the era when dishonest people would often rob mailboxes because they knew when the Social Security checks were due. So someone on SS will automatically have payments deposited into their bank account.

Becoming the Social Security Recipient's Payee
The SS Payee is the person who is legally responsible for receiving the recipient's check… but on "behalf" of the Social Security recipient. The person who becomes the payee is presumably a close family member and/or someone who has the recipient's best interest at heart. This generally happens because

the Social Security recipient has a physical and/or mental impairment that makes it advisable for someone else to help manage their finances.

The Social Security Office will have several forms that must be filled out and signed by the SS recipient. There is also a form that must be signed by the recipient's doctor that verifies that the senior is unable to handle their own financial affairs any longer.

The SS Office will also give the person who will become the payee a printout for them to take to the bank to have a new bank account opened in the senior's name. The existing bank account will not work once you become the payee. The printout from the bank with the new account information must then be returned to SS Office.

Once you are approved as the payee and the SS office makes the change, the SS payments will go to the new bank account and read:

> **SS Recipient First and Last name**
> **By "First and Last name of the payee" REP PAYEE**

This could take two or three months for payments to go to the new bank account. Don't close the old bank account until the SS payments start being deposited to the new one.

SUPPLEMENTAL SECURITY INCOME (SSI)

https://www.ssa.gov/ssi/

Administered by the Social Security Office, this supplemental payment is intended to help:

- The aged, blind, disabled people, and seniors over 65 who have limited or no income
- Provide cash to meet basic necessity for clothing, food and shelter

If you are collecting Social Security as well, there is definitely an income limit to be eligible for SSI. Suffice it to say that you have to have a 'very low' income to be eligible for SSI. And it is a very low additional amount that you receive – maybe $200 or so (varies). You will not be getting an additional $700-800 a month from SSI, and you will not qualify for SSI if you are receiving $900 or more in Social Security benefits, earned income and/or other retirement benefits.

So, do verify the income limits, but essentially you need to be practically destitute and have a "very" low income to qualify for SSI.

YES – I am repeating this from a few pages earlier because it is important and someone may read this section and not the previous one.

SSI AND ADMISSION TO A RESIDENTIAL CARE FACILITY FOR THE ELDERLY   (RCFE)

Assume these facts to be true.
- The senior is receiving a low enough amount on Social Security that they qualify for Medicaid.
- The senior is enrolled in Medicaid.
- Senior gets admitted to an Assisted Living Facility where you pay the full fee or an adjusted amount.
  THEN
- The senior can immediately apply for SSI, based on now ALREADY being in an Assisted Living Facility. The senior's income might have disqualified them for SSI before - but being admitted to the facility changes everything.
  AND – assuming they are approved
- Medicaid will then pay the balance of the senior's fees for the Assisted Living Facility. So essentially, this is a different way to get into the Medicaid Assisted Living Waiver Program because the senior is already admitted to and living in a facility.
  AND
- Once the senior is on SSI, they "automatically" qualify for Medicaid. So that means that you will no longer have to do the annual recertification that you normally do for a senior receiving Medicaid.

When I went to the Social Security office, the clerk explained the steps I describe above. Obviously, nothing is guaranteed. You apply, submit all the paperwork and the senior has to be approved for SSI. If all goes well, the senior will be approved for SSI, and receive a little more money.

Medicaid will then contact the facility to make arrangements to pay the balance of the facility fees for the senior.

PAYING THE FACILITY FEES IN THE INTERIM:

If you are able to find a facility that is willing to work with you accepting less than the full amount of the fee, that is a blessing. If not, it may be worth your while to try to save enough money between your own resources and the senior's to pay the full fee while your SSI application is pending.

Always ask if the facility has a certain amount of beds reserved for Social Security residents. This is basically a "charitable" situation where a facility is willing to accept just what the senior gets in Social Security.

As soon as you feel too old to do a thing, do it.
Margaret Deland

THE DEPARTMENT OF AGING

I think the following link is worth the price of the book!
http://www.caregiverlist.com/StateInformation.aspx

There is a Department of Aging in every single state and most provide similar services to help senior citizens maintain a better quality of life. Many of the services are designed to try to keep the senior in their home, with additional support if required. This is also generally the agency to which one would report elder abuse. Some of the services are designed for low-income seniors who are also on Medicaid. But others are intended to help any senior, regardless of income or assets.

Most of us have seen seniors in the supermarket with attendants wearing a nurse-like blouse helping the senior buy groceries. I always assumed that these were rich people who could afford to have someone follow them around the market or take them to the movies. And, more often than not, it may have been the case.

But some of these folks could be attendants who were paid – at no cost to the senior – by state agencies to assist low-income seniors. And it took me six years of caring for my father to learn that I could have been getting this financial and supportive help from the Department of Aging for years to relieve some of what I was doing.

These are some of the services offered by the California Department of Aging. It is almost identical to most states.

- Adult Protective Services
- Family Caregiver Support Program

- **In-Home Supportive Services (IHSS)**
- Health Insurance Counseling and Advocacy Program
- Long-Term Care Ombudsman
- Multipurpose Senior Services Program
- Nutrition Services
- Provider Services
- Public Guardian - Conservator
- Senior Community Service Employment Program
- Senior Information and Assistance

IN-HOME SUPPORT SERVICES (IHSS)

The service I want to concentrate on is the **In-Home Support Services (IHSS)**. IHSS pays a helper (provider), which could be someone you hire OR *you* as the caregiver for a variety of support services that help the senior live a better quality of life in their own home.

In California in 2017, the hourly rate of pay was $10.50, and a senior could qualify for up to 280 hours a month. The number of hours a month that the senior is allotted by the Dept. of Aging is determined by the amount of care they need. Be mindful that you will receive a 1099 IRS tax form at the end of the year for this income, and it is reportable to the IRS.

People qualify for IHSS services if they:
- Are 65 years of age or more, disabled or blind.
- **Have a Medicaid (or Medi-Cal) eligibility determination.**
- **Have a functional impairment and are at risk for out of home care placement.**
- Have a need for IHSS services in order to remain safely at home. This could mean they need help bathing, getting in and out of bed, taking medication, cooking, etc.
- Physically reside in the United States.

- Live at home or an abode of their own choosing (acute care hospital, long-term care facilities, and licensed community care facilities are not considered your "own home").
- Submit a completed Health Care Certification form.

I have highlighted two of the most important requirements for IHSS. The senior must also be on Medicaid or eligible to receive Medicaid. And there has to be some condition, some impairment that qualifies them for a residential care facility, except that the senior (and you the caregiver perhaps) wants to stay in the home.

When my dad was approved for these services, he was living with me and my husband. So, it doesn't have to be that the senior is in their "own" home, but living in someone's home where they are cared for and it is considered their primary residence. In-Home Support Services are not available if the senior is moved to a residential care facility.

THE STEPS FOR YOU TO QUALIFY TO BECOME A SERVICE PROVIDER and FOR THE SENIOR TO QUALIFY FOR SERVICES:

RECIPIENT (THE PERSON NEEDING CARE)
- Call the Department of Aging and make them aware that you are interested in In-Home Support Services. The Dept. of Aging will arrange for a social worker to come to your home to do an assessment of the senior and the services they need.
- *This visit is critical* because in addition to them assessing the senior, the caregiver (assuming you live with them) will need to detail the help that they provide the senior. This visit will determine how many hours a month the

senior qualifies for care and exactly which services they get based on what you do for them. <u>So be specific</u>. There are little things you may do for the senior and not think about. But these tasks could get added to the hours the senior is allotted by the state. My father's pride had him giving the social worker different answers that I corrected.

- There will be a form for the senior's doctor to complete.
- These services are FOR the senior. So the senior will receive a letter detailing how many hours and minutes for which they are eligible, and it will specify the services the senior has been approved for (see list below).
- Later, The Department of Aging will provide you with a list of approved care providers (or ask for one). You should follow the suggested guidelines on interviewing potential providers (in a public place – not your home) and pick a provider that suits the senior and you. You can always change providers.

STEPS TO **<u>QUALIFY AS A PROVIDER</u>** OF SERVICES:

- For you to qualify as a service provider, you will need to get fingerprinted and then (in California) go for a one-time four-hour training / orientation session that explains the IHSS program.
- Once your fingerprinting and orientation are successfully completed, you will be assigned a provider payroll number and timesheets, which you will submit every two weeks for the services you provide the senior. You will sign this time sheet, as will the senior (verifying that you provided the services). These payments can be retroactive based on the date the senior is approved.

- If you have Power of Attorney and the senior is incapacitated and unable to sign, you can sign the payroll form for them. There are serious fines for fraud, so be honest!
- You are given a travel allowance ONLY if you are providing services for two or more seniors and have to travel between locations to provide services.
- As of this printing, the hourly rate of pay in California is $10.50.

Your Department of Aging will explain the program in full detail. Please refer to its website or to the literature you receive. These are some of the California contact numbers.

- IHSS Timesheet Issues/Questions: (866) 376-7066
- IHSS Program Integrity: (916) 651-3494
- IHSS Program policy: (916) 651-5350
- IHSS Quality Assurance: (916) 651-3494
- IHSS Training: IHSS-Training@dss.ca.gov, (916) 651-3494

LINK TO CALIFORNIA COUNTY IHSS OFFICES:
http://www.cdss.ca.gov/inforesources/County-IHSS-Offices

IHSS SPECIFIC SENIOR SERVICES:
Whether you are trying to get an assistant to help you care for the senior or you decide to apply to get paid for providing this service yourself, <u>following are some of the services the California Department of Aging pays a provider.</u>

For each one of these services, the social worker will allot a certain amount of minutes for the action and multiply how many hours or minutes the provider is allotted per day, week and month to help the senior.

- Prepare meals, meal clean-up, shopping for food
- Other shopping or errands
- Routine laundry
- Respiration assistance (inhalers and other machines)
- Bowel, bladder care
- Feeding
- Routine bed, bath, dressing
- Ambulation (help with walking, including getting in and out of vehicles)
- Transferring (help moving in/out of bed, on/off seats)
- Bathing, oral hygiene, grooming
- Rubbing skin, repositioning
- Help with prosthesis
- Accompanying to/from medical appointments
- Heavy cleaning, yard hazard abatements, removing ice, snow

As I described things I did for my father on a daily basis, things I didn't think about, the social worker marked that as another service for which IHSS would pay a hired provider or me. So before this visit, think very carefully about every single thing you do for the senior. If the senior gets food stamps and you shop separately for them that is a separate set of tasks.

Also, if the senior's condition worsens you should contact IHSS to have them reevaluated to get allotted more hours.

Adult Protective Services: Abuse
Assuming you are well intentioned, you will not overtly do anything to harm the senior in your care. But it helps to be aware of what is considered senior abuse because some of these

are not things you might consider to be abusive. Be aware so you don't wind up getting reported for something you never considered abuse. Also, if you see these forms of abusive behaviors in others you know what you should report. This is list of what is considered abusive behavior on the Alzheimer's Association website:

Physical: causing physical pain or injury

Emotional: verbal assaults, threats of abuse, harassment and intimidation

Neglect: failure to provide necessities, including food, clothing, shelter, medical care or a safe environment

Confinement: restraining or isolating the person

Financial: the misuse or withholding of the person's financial resources (money, property) to his or her disadvantage or the advantage of someone else

Sexual abuse: touching, fondling or any sexual activity when the person is unable to understand, unwilling to consent, threatened or physically forced

Willful deprivation: willfully denying the person medication, medical care, food, shelter or physical assistance, and thereby exposing the individual with Alzheimer's to the risk of physical, mental or emotional harm

Self neglect: Due to lack of insight and cognitive changes, a person with Alzheimer's may be unable to safely and adequately provide for day-to-day needs, and may be at risk for harm, falls, wandering and/or malnutrition.

TRANSPORTATION SERVICES
www.adaride.com

While every state has funds set aside in various senior programs to help defray or totally eliminate the cost of public transportation for seniors, this can also come down to a county-by-county benefit. For more functional seniors, this could involve a bus coming to pick them up at home to take them shopping, to the mall, or to doctor's visits. The caregiver will need to determine how clear thinking the senior is as to whether they can travel safely alone.

I suggest starting with your local Department of Aging, social worker, Dept. of Transportation (buses and trains) or even hospital. Just because you are registered for Ride Share services in L.A. does not mean that your registration will apply if you move 40 minutes away to West Covina or an hour away to Rancho Cucamonga. It is probably the same in each state.

You will want to check with the agency that handles this registration and make sure of the coverage area. That means in what cities, counties or how many miles from your home is covered for senior transportation.

Southern California has ADARide and some counties have a Transportation Reimbursement Information Project (TRIP), which provides mileage reimbursement for volunteer drivers.

ASSISTED LIVING FACILITY PLACEMENT

And

SENIOR HOUSING OPTIONS

I really feel better about aging at 86, than I did at 70.
Donald Hall

PLACEMENT and HOUSING CHOICES

SOME PLACES FOR MOM or DAD
There are a lot of TV ads about agencies that can help you with senior placement for your parents. I am certain that this is a great service. I called the number for one of the most recognized of those TV commercials. The main thing you need to know is that they do not provide placement referrals for people on Medicaid. So if you are low-income, and struggling to figure out how to pay for senior care, your choices will be limited with this call.

WHAT'S IN A NAME?
Residential Care Facilities for the Elderly (RCFE), Assisted Living Facility, Nursing Homes, Senior Citizen Homes, Rehab Centers, Senior Independent Living Complexes or Communities, and Board & Care Facility

There is a big difference between all of the above, though most of us tend to say "Nursing Home" and think that term covers just about everything that means the senior is not living with you. Each state might have a slightly different name for these non-medical adult care facilities for the disabled or elderly.

AND… just like there are "mixed use" buildings that have apartments or condos at the top of a building and a Trader Joe's, convenience store, pizza joint or a pharmacy downstairs, there are senior buildings that are mixed use. By this I mean that one building (like The Grove in Riverside, California) can combine independent retirement living, assisted living and even skilled nursing / rehabilitation services in one building or several adjoining buildings.

Residential Care Facilities for the Elderly (RCFE)
(See the Medicaid Assisted Living Waiver also)

These can be called Assisting Living Facilities, Alzheimer's Care Center, Board and Care Facilities and some Rehab Facilities. Again, the titles may vary per state.

These are non-medical facilities that provide a level of care that includes assistance with activities of daily living like bathing, grooming and meals. There are skilled professionals on site (not necessarily nurses unless it is a building with mixed services).

Some states, like Florida, were a mecca for retirees decades ago. And many families in these states are now in financial crises trying to find affordable long-term facility care for the huge amount of infirm seniors, many with Alzheimer's.

RCFEs in California are licensed by the State Department of Social Services, Community Care Licensing Division (CCL). CCL keeps an updated list right on its home page of facilities that have open beds, though they may not necessarily be a Medicaid bed.
http://www.cdss.ca.gov/inforesources/Community-Care-Licensing

Skilled Nursing Facility, Convalescent Homes, Nursing Homes and Rehab Centers are different and provide some degree of medical care. They are licensed by other agencies.

The forms to have your senior admitted to an Assisted Living Facility or RCFE may include:
- The facility's application

- The physician's report (that justifies why they need to be in such a facility)
- Medication Profile
- Advanced Medical Care Directive

Payment for RCFEs can come from one or a combination of the individual's or family's personal finances or a Medicaid Assisted Living Waiver Program. People on SSI have an easier time having their RCFE fees paid for through Medicaid.

Assisted Living Facilities

This term pretty much speaks for itself. These are residential care facilities that can house seniors, the disabled or Alzheimer's patients. It means that the senior might have their own apartment, a private room or a shared room with another senior. But to some degree or another they need 'assistance' with certain things that will help them live more comfortably (dressing, bathing, administration of medication, walking, getting in and out of bed, etc.). These are still considered "Residential Care Facilities."

The monthly fees for such facilities probably vary quite a bit per state. In California, they can run from $2800 on the low end to $6,000 or more a month for the high-end facilities. As a wild guess, I would say that a "good" facility will cost about $4,000-5,000 a month. A news feature on facilities in Florida seemed to indicate $4,000 a month to be the low end.

Clearly, this tells you that the prices can have a huge variance according the state, county, city, neighborhood and the quality of care and amenities provided.

Board & Care Facilities

These facilities are generally for lower-income residents, but may or may not take Medicaid. Some Board and Care Facilities can have as few as six residents in a building that can be like a private home and larger facilities can have hundreds. In the larger facilities, they sometimes have separate areas for patients with memory issues, behavioral problems or limited financial resources.

In Southern California, a really inexpensive one where the senior will be sharing a room and bathroom with someone else could be about $1,500 to $2,600 a month. That's the cheap end of the spectrum. If that's the fee for an inexpensive care facility, let your imagination run wild with what the better ones cost. Of course, this will vary by state and county.

Staying at HOME

Let's face it: Most of us hope to stay in our own homes as long as possible while we age. Some seniors look forward to living in a gated senior community where they never again have to worry about loud music from the neighbor next door or crying babies.

But despite whatever the environment, when people have built memories where they live, raised their children in a place and loved in that place, most want to stay there as they grow older. So, if there is a possibility that you can safely leave the senior in their home and get the services to help them live comfortably, do so. And, in weighing the cost of a facility, one might want to consider if it is cheaper to move a caregiver into the home.

With that in mind, this latest revision of the book has prompted me to add a section on reverse mortgages as a way to keep the senior in their home.

Reverse Mortgages

I am not a fan of reverse mortgages for a lot of reasons that could easily involve an entirely different book. I am currently writing an article about the pitfalls of reverse mortgages that might be available online by the time you purchase this book. But as I think of the many questions I've been asked in the past few months since first publishing, I realize that a reverse mortgage is worth mentioning in terms of a way for the elderly to stay in their homes and possibly maintain a greater sense of what is familiar to them. It is important that you research this thoroughly and not just rely on the handsome actors in TV commercials and glossy brochures to oversimplify "all" that is involved with a reverse mortgage.

First, let me say both the good and bad in a nutshell:
- For seniors 62 and older who own their own home, a reverse mortgage allows you to access the equity in your home. You can get a lump sum from the lender against that equity and/or a line of credit that you can occasionally dip into.
- The lender pays off your current mortgage (becoming your new mortgage holder) and you continue to live in your home - mortgage free – until you and your spouse* die. At that point, your children can still inherit your home as long as they pay off the reverse mortgage lender.
- Downside: While you are not paying a mortgage anymore, there is interest piling up on the back end of the reverse mortgage loan that eats away at the value of your property.
- Downside: the reverse mortgage comes with sizable 'closing' costs just like when you are buying a house or refinancing.

*Spouse: If your spouse is not 62, in order for the loan to proceed the younger spouse will have to sign over their interest in the deed to the house to the older spouse who qualifies for the reverse mortgage. That is a tricky thing to do – signing over your legal rights to your home, and it is worth serious consideration, especially if you are not in a community property state. Check with the reverse mortgage lender as to whether the younger spouse still gets to stay in the house when the qualifying senior passes away. It's possible they might not.

What I did: A couple of months after our reverse mortgage went through, we put the deed back in both our names. This was perfectly legit. My name was "not" on the reverse mortgage loan, but I was back on the deed. As I said, there is a lot involved with reverse mortgages.

Mobile/Manufactured Homes: If your mobile home was built after 1990, you may still qualify for a reverse mortgage depending on the lender. Much has to do with the condition of the home, the land and the foundation of the home. Check the link below in terms of HUD's requirements for mobile home foundations as one part of qualifying.
https://www.hud.gov/program_offices/administration/hudclips/guidebooks/4930.3G
I "do not" in any way endorse this lender, but the following is an excellent article detailing what is involved for mobile homes to qualify for a reverse mortgage.
https://reverse.mortgage/manufactured-home

For the purposes of staying in your home when you may be feeling the signs of old age physically and mentally, freeing up the money that you once paid for a monthly mortgage gives you extra capital to pay a caregiver to come into your home or move in so you have 24/7 care. Again, this is something you and your family would need to research carefully. There is a lot involved with moving a stranger into your home. Make wise choices.

But assuming you find a credible, caring person whom you and your family are comfortable with, think of this solution. You provide this live-in caregiver with room and board. These are the two most expensive items on a person's budget – rent and food. That means that with the money you are saving them on room and board that you should be able to pay them a moderate monthly fee as a salary. Make sure you have your loved ones collaborate with you on a contract, arrangements for days and times off where other family members might be able to come into the home to relieve your live-in caregiver.

The flip side of this is that the caregiver should fully understand what they are signing up for in terms of caring for an elderly person, possibly with dementia, who might have grooming and bathing needs or might need to be assisted physically. Whether you go through an agency or perform your own due diligence is another matter.

The upshot of this is that the senior stays in their home. And for your own peace of mind, if these are your parents, invest in a nanny cam or other visual security measures. These days, that is just simple to do.

Other suggestions:
These are some of the typical and not so typical places that can also help the senior who wants to stay in their own home.

Colleges/Universities
Do some research and find out whether any of your local universities have outreach programs where the students spend time with seniors.

Faith-Based Organizations
Many places have outreach programs that involve going out into the community. Check with either your church, neighboring churches or other faith-based organizations to see what programs they have for seniors. This may include visits to seniors in the home to check on them.

In-Home Support Services
Once the senior has qualified for Medicaid, they are eligible for these extra services, usually under the auspices of the Department of Aging. Once the senior is approved to receive this – based on income-level and being on Medicaid – they are given a certain number of hours a month, and a provider who has gone through fingerprinting and training. See the chapter on the Department of Aging for full details.

Meals on Wheels
No senior need go hungry. This program is generally run by the Department of Aging and delivers meals to the senior's home either free or at a very low cost.

Nursing Homes or Rehabilitation Facilities
Placing someone in a "nursing home" has generally been considered the catch-all phrase that meant you had placed the senior in a home. But technically a nursing home is just that – a care facility where the senior receives "skilled nursing care" because of some physical condition that requires them to be

there. Generally, a doctor has to issue the order for someone to go to a skilled nursing home or rehab facility. This care can be provided by a team of medical professionals. It could be that the senior broke a hip and needs rehab until they return home. Or they could be recovering from a heart attack, surgery or a stroke. Nursing Homes are licensed by a different agency than residential care facilities.

Medicare allows for 100 days a year in a nursing home. The hospital or doctors may try to rush the senior out of there sooner. But be vocal and advocate for more time if you or your caregiver do not feel the senior is stable or improved. Also, the hospital will want to know – for sure – that the senior has a place to which they can return before the doctor approves the nursing home placement. That means an address at either their own home, their caregiver's home or a residential care facility.

Kaiser Permanente: and Residential Care Facilities
Kaiser is one of the largest and most respected HMOs in the country. During the last few months caring for my father in my home, I learned that Kaiser has its own system of helping its members get placed in an Assisted Living Facility. The department, at least in California, is called their "Senior Care Connection."

You will want to make sure that in addition to Medicare, the senior is signed up for Medicaid as well – assuming they are eligible. But there could be circumstances where Kaiser assists even if it is not a Medicaid recipient. The team at Kaiser utilizes all available insurance coverage to help make the placement, working directly with connections they have at various elderly care facilities. Make absolutely certain that for wherever you physically reside that your Medicaid coverage is in the same county. Confer with your doctor because he or she will have to make the referral to the Senior Care Connections Department at Kaiser for them to put you or the senior in your care in their system to start looking for a facility.

Senior Living Buildings, Complexes, Communities, etc.

Essentially, this is a community where the main requirement is that you be 55 or older to live there. Most of them also have limitations on people under 55 staying with you for longer than two weeks at a time or for a certain amount of days or months a year. The point is to keep it a senior community and not have the kids or grandkids move in with you. Some of the communities require that you be 62 or over.

These could be a million-dollar, gated community with homes on a golf course or a subsidized building that basically has Section 8 income limitations. The range of possibilities is limitless. Fancy buildings, lousy buildings, mobile home parks (no longer PC to call them trailer parks) that are beautiful and well maintained and the ones that are deplorable. There are subsidized senior living apartment buildings that are a block from the beach and some in neighborhoods where every other house has iron security bars on the windows.

There are some federally subsidized senior buildings that provide a range of services to its residents – social worker, entertainment, trips, etc. But the main point of these buildings is that most are independent living… meaning that the seniors are self-sufficient and do not require care.

HUD – Housing Urban Development helps apartment owners offer reduced rents to low-income tenants. Some buildings are considered Public Housing, whereas others are privately owned buildings where the landlord gets massive tax credits for making all or part of the building low-income.

I am not familiar with other states, but I was shocked to learn that in Los Angeles–even though some of these low-income subsidized senior buildings might be in areas where you might fear for your safety on a daily basis—there are also many that are in expensive parts of town. That includes Santa Monica, a block from the beach or with an ocean view. *For real.*

The important thing is to do your research, check out the building and the neighborhood, make some calls, find out whether the building is accepting applications and how long you would be on the waiting list. I called one building in a very nice section of downtown L.A. where the waiting list was only 1.5 years for a one-bedroom apartment that would cost about $1100 a month. Another apartment building in Santa Monica had a five-year waiting list and another in the same area had a 15-year waiting list. I asked several times if they really meant 15 years. They did.

My husband and I went to look at one of the apartments. It was shocking how small it was – a one bedroom for $1100 that was barely 500 square feet. But if you are a senior on an extremely fixed, poverty-level income and a Section 8 voucher is not available to you, this could be a good option. Being able to move into a building where you know that rent increases are minor and you will not have to worry about screaming babies, might make this a good choice despite the smallness of the apartments. This is the ultimate in downsizing. The rent is based on your income, so if your income is 'extremely low' the rent will be lower.

Go to: www.hud.gov
- SCROLL DOWN TO the "Find Rental Assistance" link
- From there, select your housing option to search.
- NEED HELP: has a choice to search through privately owned buildings
- LOCAL RENTAL INFORMATION: has a link that will guide you to properties with low-income housing credits (these are the buildings that have discounted rents pretty much in the whole building)

Do your homework, visit the area, tour the building and get on multiple waiting lists. You never know which one might open up first.

CAREGIVER RESOURCES and Issues

As I said at the start, caring for an elderly person with declining physical and mental abilities is stressful. It's not that it "can be" stressful. It is stressful. Whether you ask another member of your family for help, find paid services or get someone from your church to help you… make sure you take care of yourself. Get help and take a break.

Common Caregiver Problems
- Depression
-
- Anxiety (guilt, sadness, dread, worry)
-
- Access to information and finding resources
-
- Fatigue (sleep problems)
-
- Employment problems (missed work)
-
- Adjusting to the 'new normal' of dealing with the elderly, especially one with dementia

Respite Care:
This literally means a break or mini vacation from being a caregiver. If there is a family member or trusted friend or neighbor with whom you can entrust your senior's care for a few hours a week, do so. Overnight? Even better. That little break will allow you to recharge your batteries, clear your head, and indulge in some "me" time so you can continue to provide

quality loving care. But it will also reinvigorate you so you don't feel trapped. And if you are married or have a significant other, you definitely need a respite break so your entire life is not centered around elder care issues 24/7.

If you do not have someone who will do this for free (or maybe for a Starbucks or movie gift card), there are so many services available. And many are free or discounted. Respite care comes in basically three forms:

Caregiver Resources – Private Pay

The following selective Private Pay Caregiver Resources (Southern California) may not make sense for regular, long-term care. But if all else fails in terms of other free or low-priced services that you access, it might be worth your time to gather the money to pay for a few hours or a day off just to give yourself a break. Prices can vary greatly and may be between $15 to $50 an hour, and the agency may have a two or four-hour minimum. Call the ones below or others you find for details.

Affordable Companion Care – 800-562-5994
www.companioncarecalifornia.com

Provides companion care services throughout Southern California that can help the patient with cooking, cleaning, shopping, etc.
24-hour care can start at $190 and there are hourly rates as well.
Angels of the Valley Senior Home Care 951-927-7428
Inland Empire / Riverside County
American Companion & Caregivers 909-373-8670
Rancho Cucamonga

Nurse Next Door – 866-279-9991
San Bernardino / Riverside / Orange / L.A.

Once again, I am not endorsing one type of care over another; nor am I endorsing any of these agencies. Continue to do your own research in the city/state where you live. You may be able to get respite care through some state agencies as well. We cover respite care through Hospice in the next chapter.

Chronic Therapist Elderly Cost
Dressing Disabilities Assisted Living
Premiums Physicians Insurance LONG Caregiver Nursing Home Managed
TERM On Site Healthcare
Work Age Hygiene CARE Residential Personal Expense Older LTC Custodial Hospice Needs
Supervised Seniors Nurse Doctor
Paid Health Facility Activities Taxes

HOSPICE CARE

National Hospice and Palliative Care Organization
https://www.nhpco.org/

Hospice usually refers to "end of life" care to make a person comfortable when they are dealing with a terminal disease or they have chronic pain. But there are other situations under which a person might be placed on hospice. It could be because they are so elderly and feeble that death seems imminent to the point where their doctor agrees that they warrant hospice care.

Years ago, almost all hospice care was done in a facility that was similar to or part of a nursing home. My grandmother was placed in a hospice facility in Philly in 1968 after three surgeries when she continued to waste away from cancer. Patients went to hospice facilities knowing that it was end of life care. The families also understood that pretty much everyone there had some terminal illness and their care required more than the family could handle.

While I am sure there are still hospice facilities, today most hospice agencies, hospitals and doctors try to keep the person in their home. Then they provide you with extra help from a Hospice Agency to assist the family in caring for the ill or infirm patient. The level of care depends on how much assistance the sick person needs.

I asked my father's doctor to place Dad on hospice. His doctor understood that Dad's fragility and ailing condition were more than I could handle. The last couple of weeks with us, Dad couldn't walk and my husband and I had to lift him in and out of his wheelchair. Every time we touched him, he said he was in pain.

When my dad's doctor agreed that he could be placed on hospice care, it was not what I expected. I thought Dad would be taken to a facility. Instead, a team of people started showing up on our doorstep: social workers, nurses, and attendants who were willing to bathe him and check him physically. I was unprepared for the sudden intrusion of all these people in my home. So you need to be prepared to lose your privacy to a large degree. And, if you are at all conscientious, this will also force you to be tidier and mindful of your house cleaning habits!

While I was, at first, disappointed that they did not take Dad to a facility, it was a huge help to suddenly have all this extra support.

You can get hospice care if you have <u>Medicare Part A (Hospital Insurance)</u> AND meet all of these conditions:
- Your hospice doctor and your regular doctor or nurse practitioner (if you have one) certify that you're terminally ill (you're expected to live 6 months or less).
- You accept palliative care (for comfort) instead of care to cure your illness.
- You sign a statement choosing hospice care instead of other Medicare-covered treatments for your terminal illness and related conditions. (medicare.gov)

Make sure you check the medicare.gov site for some of the things that Medicare does "not" cover while on hospice.

And, once again, assuming the senior is on Medicaid, the hospice agency will get their funding through a combination of these sources: Medicare, Medicaid and private donations directly to the hospice agency in a lot of cases. It is another reason why having Medicare and Medicaid increases your coverage of services.

Even though Dad had a regular doctor, the hospice agency had their own doctors who became part of his medical care team. They could prescribe medications (free of charge) in coordination with the medications Dad was already taking, but also in addition to what his doctor prescribed if the hospice doctor felt it was warranted.

Hospice care did not impact Dad's eligibility for <u>In Home Support Services (IHSS)</u> through the Department of Aging. Be mindful of IHSS services you are being paid for that hospice may take over. For instance, if you are getting paid to bathe the person and hospice takes that over, you will want to deduct the minutes or hours from your IHSS timesheet. Remember that you do not want to commit fraud with the Department of Aging by submitting time for tasks you no longer perform.

The following additional information is from the medicare.gov site:
Hospice care is usually given in your home, but it also may be covered in a hospice inpatient facility. Depending on your terminal illness and related conditions, the plan of care your hospice team creates can include any or all of these services:

- Doctor's services
- Nursing care
- Medical equipment (like wheelchairs or walkers)
- Medical supplies (like bandages and catheters)
- Prescription drugs for symptom control or pain relief
- Hospice aide and homemaker services
- Physical therapy services

- Occupational therapy services
- Speech-language pathology services
- Social work services
- Dietary counseling
- Grief and loss counseling for you and your family
- Short-term inpatient care (for pain and symptom management)
- Short term respite care

Any other Medicare-covered services needed to manage your pain and other symptoms related to your terminal illness and related conditions, as recommended by your hospice team. Here are the services you can expect that we experienced with my dad's care on hospice:

- A social worker will be assigned to your case and this person will become your point person for coordinating all your senior's care. They will also make periodic checks to your home to make sure the senior is being well cared for.
- Nurses or nurse practitioners may visit your home a couple of times a week to take the senior's vitals, check on any physical impairments or how they are coping with their pain management.
- If you require help bathing the person, attendants can come in on a schedule that you set up to bathe them. According to the gender of the senior and caregiver, this can be a sensitive area of care with which neither of you is comfortable. I was blessed to have a husband who began to help with showering Dad. But it was quite a relief to have two hospice care workers come in and do this.

- **E-KIT or COMFORT KIT MEDICATIONS**
  (Emergency supply): The first nurse who came by our
  house dropped off a box with packets of medications that
  were meant for us to have on hand so we wouldn't have
  to run to the drugstore or call in a prescription. A
  Comfort Kit can include the following:
  - **Morphine liquid** — used to treat pain and shortness
    of breath
  - **Ativan (Lorazepam)** — can be used to treat anxiety,
    nausea or insomnia
  - **Atropine drops** — used to treat wet respirations,
    also known as the death rattle
  - **Haldol (Haloperidol)** — can treat agitation and
    terminal restlessness
  - **Compazine (prochlorperazine)** — in either pill or
    rectal suppository form, this medication is used to
    treat nausea and vomiting
  - **Phenergan (promethazine)** — an anti-emetic like
    Compazine, Phenergan used for nausea and vomiting
  - **Dulcolax suppositories (Bisacodyl)** — rectal
    suppositories to treat constipation
  - **Senna** — a plant-based laxative
  - **Fleet Enema** — used to treat constipation if other
    treatments are ineffective
- RESPITE CARE: By the time Dad was put on hospice,
  we had had a very stressful time with him as his mobility
  and mental status both deteriorated rapidly. I was at my
  wits end, and the social worker asked if I would like a
  few days of respite care. Respite is covered in the section
  on Caregiver Resources. But recall that this places the
  senior in either a nursing home or assisted living facility
  for a brief stay outside your home. Our hospice agency
  placed Dad in a beautiful nearby assisted living facility

for five days free of charge. Sometimes you can pay a reasonable fee directly to the facility to arrange for a couple of extra nights.

    a. If the **hospice** team determines that you need short-term inpatient or respite care services that they arrange, Medicare will cover the stay in the facility. You may have to pay a small copayment for the respite stay. Care you get as a hospital outpatient (like in an **emergency** room), care you get as a hospital inpatient ... (medicare.gov)

- EQUIPMENT and SUPPLIES: In the time that Dad was on hospice, we received:
  - a. adult undergarments, bed pads
  - b. shampoo, lotions, cleansing gels, plastic gloves
  - c. a shower chair
  - d. an adjustable hospital bed
  - e. a wheelchair, a walker
  - f. a hospital tray for him to be able to eat in bed
  - g. This massive arched crane equipment that was supposed to help us get him from his wheelchair over to the bed (and avoid us having to lift him).

Hospice care, as you can see, could be an incredible help to you and your family when caring for an elderly person who is fading fast, experiences chronic pain or someone who is terminally ill. That is why it is important to establish a good relationship with your senior's doctor. A period of time on hospice care could give the caregiver the additional resources to help them maintain their own emotional and physical health.

LONG TERM CARE OMBUDSMAN SERVICES

An ombudsman is a person who serves as a mediator, investigator or watchdog. Universities have ombudsmen who help bridge any differences or aid communication between students and faculty, or between staff and administrators. Yes, there are women who do this. I couldn't find the gender-neutral term.

In senior care, the long-term care ombudsman acts as an advocate for the senior, coordinating with the family to make sure that the senior is treated well in whatever residential care facility in which they are placed.

This is most generally an office within the Department of Aging. My personal opinion is that if you are going to make any complaints against a residential care facility to the Ombudsman that you should feel sure they are based on a solid concern. When my one sister Annette was in a nursing home after a stroke, my other sister, Gina, constantly complained to the nurses and administrators about everything to do with Annette's care. Some of it was valid, but some was just Gina complaining. I finally said to her once, "With the amount of grief you give those people, do you ever think of how they treat our sister when you aren't around?" She lightened up a bit. There is a reason they say you can catch more flies with honey.

You have every right – and should - voice any valid concerns, and show the facility that you are present in your loved one's life. But do not make false complaints or you don't know how that might come back to negatively impact the senior.

The following information is directly from the California Department of Aging site:

Overview
The California State Long-Term Care Ombudsman Program is authorized by the federal <u>Older Americans Act</u> and its State companion, the <u>Older Californians Act</u>.

The primary responsibility of the program is to investigate and endeavor to resolve complaints made by, or on behalf of, individual residents in long-term care facilities. These facilities include nursing homes, residential care facilities for the elderly, and assisted living facilities. The Long-Term Care Ombudsman Program investigates elder abuse complaints in long-term care facilities and in residential care facilities for the elderly.

The goal of the State Long-Term Care Ombudsman Program is to advocate for the rights of all residents of long-term care facilities.

The Ombudsman's advocacy role takes two forms:
1) to receive and resolve individual complaints and issues by, or on behalf of, these residents; and 2) to pursue resident advocacy in the long-term care system, its laws, policies, regulations, and administration through public education and consensus building.
2) Residents or their family members can file a complaint directly with the local Long-Term Care Ombudsman or by calling the CRISIS line.

All long-term care facilities are required to post, in a conspicuous location, the phone number for the local Ombudsman office and the Statewide CRISIS line number 800-231-4024. This CRISIS line is available 24 hours a day, 7 days a week to take calls and refer complaints from residents.

The Long-Term Care Ombudsman Program is a community-supported program. Volunteers are an integral part of this program. The OSLTCO and its 35 local Ombudsman Program Coordinators are responsible for recruiting, training, and supervising the volunteer Ombudsman representatives. https://www.aging.ca.gov/programs/ltcop/

I spoke with an Ombudsman shortly before Dad's last facility placement – somewhere between me being very frazzled and the hospice care. He was a fine example of someone who seemed destined to do this kind of work. He was kind, caring and provided me with good information about his office.

Do not go gentle into that good night,
Old age should burn and rave at close of day;
Rage, rage against the dying of the light.
[. . .]   Dylan Thomas

circa 1947

circa 1963

World's Fair 1964

My husband Rob, me and Dad at the birth of my grandson, 2014

You get old and you realize there are no answers, just stories.

Garrison Keillor, Pontoon

PLANNING FOR YOUR ELDER YEARS

My own pittance of a retirement makes me the last person capable of telling you how to plan for a comfortable retirement. But I will say this: start early and put aside a little something, no matter how modest an amount. Live as frugally as possible to try to save money towards retirement.

If you wait until you are already in your late 50s or 60s, it's hard to turn around a lifetime of not preparing for your retirement income. But whatever you can save is important. Here are a few thoughts.

1. Medicaid: Apply for it if your income is low enough.
2. Extra Work: Find some little stress-free way to earn a few extra bucks a month.
3. Look into subsidized senior housing that will at least ease the burden financially in terms of allowing you to live in an apartment building where your rent won't be going up by huge chunks annually.
4. Section 8: If you are eligible for Medicaid, chances are you might also qualify for a Section 8 voucher. Again, that will allow you to live somewhere affordable. I learned recently from a woman I know on Section 8 that you can apply for the voucher anywhere in the U.S. (including the U.S. Virgin Islands). It does not have to be in the city or county you live. The caveat is that if you are approved, you have to live in that area (the county/city for which you were approved) for at least a year. After that, the voucher is portable and you can use it anywhere in the U.S. where the landlord will accept the Section 8 voucher. – BIG CAUTION: That is second

hand information. Check with Section 8 to make sure that is accurate. But my good friend did "exactly" what I just described here.

5. <u>Senior Citizen Centers</u>: These places not only provide a wonderful social outlet for seniors with all kinds of activities and free or inexpensive lunches, but often are a resource for great information to help seniors with all kinds of services.

6. <u>Save your money</u>. It might be too late to build up a strong 401K or other retirement plan beyond a certain age, but your private funds can help with some of your care.

7. <u>Reverse Mortgages</u>. I've already discussed in the section on housing options why this might be a good choice for some seniors. The simplest version of my suggestion here, after you have done all your research and discussed with your family, is that entering into a reverse mortgage might be a way for you to stay in your home and pay for someone to come help you in your home with the money you used to pay for the mortgage. You should undertake full due diligence before engaging in this option.

<u>The Buddy System</u>:

If you have a strong social network (a live one with actual humans – not Facebook and Twitter), you might want to think about moving in with another senior to help each other out. It could be that your combined financial resources and physical/mental abilities could aid each other. That, combined with the many services available to seniors, could keep you both out of a senior residential facility and in your own space longer. Take a page from your grandkids! Young people just starting out think nothing of getting a roommate to share their living space and expenses. Why not think about this as a senior? Where one of you lacks the ability to do something, the other might be able to help. And one or both of you might still qualify for In-Home Support Services through the Department of Aging.

Here are a few links to companies that specialize in pairing seniors with each other. While I don't personally endorse any one of these, they might be a helpful resource.

https://www.seniorly.com/resources/articles/consider-having-a-senior-roommate

https://www.silvernest.com/

http://www.seniorhomeshares.com/

"Some day you will be old enough to start reading fairy tales again."

C.S. Lewis

FINAL ARRANGEMENTS

Everyone has to make their own decisions based on spiritual, personal and religious beliefs. But a "cheap" funeral with a metal casket can cost $8,000 and cremation $800. Some people object to cremation for religious reasons, and I respect that. The choice is yours and your family's decision to make. It is something you might want to discuss with the senior while they can still make decisions. Here are just a few things to consider cutting down on the cost of a funeral: Most of this is referenced directly from the Moneytalksnews website.

- <u>Shop around</u> for the best funeral prices and ask that they itemize the charges
- There is such a thing as a <u>'direct' burial</u> that takes place soon after the death.
- The silk-lined mahogany casket is more for your comfort. There are many <u>inexpensive caskets</u> as low as $1,000. (*You could always think of getting that pine box and painting it pretty colors.*)
- If you choose cremation, you can cut down on costs and <u>buy your own urn</u>. And even if the person is cremated, you can still buy a burial plot if that is important to your family. There is a funny scene from the movie "The Bucket List" where Jack Nicholson puts his friend (Morgan Freeman's) ashes in a Chock Full of Nuts coffee can. It was a private joke between them about which was the more quality coffee.
- Consider a <u>"green" or "natural" burial</u> that does not use all the toxic embalming fluids and a very inexpensive (less than $100) biodegradable shroud). There are very few of these cemeteries around the county. Do your own

research or see the natural burial company - www.naturalburialcompany.com/

- Hold the funeral at home: There was a time when this was the norm. We've all seen movies of the coffin set up in the living room for the viewing. This is about as "old school" as it gets. For advice, check out: Threshold Care Circle for workshops www.thresholdcarecircle.org/
- And… check out The Home Funeral Alliance: http://homefuneralalliance.org/ Find guides on the legal requirements for each state.
- Choose a home burial: Again, once a common practice for people with land to have a small family cemetery. Find out the state laws on this. (*There are definitely some states where if you have enough land they allow this.*)
- Bring your own flowers. Hit up Trader Joe's or your local supermarket or a friend's backyard. You are not 'required' to use a florist.
- Hold the service at a church or mosque. When you see the detailed costs for a funeral, part of the cost is the use of the funeral home's space.
- Make the repast after the service a potluck. If available try using a church hall or somewhere else inexpensive if you don't have a suitable space in someone's home.
- Veterans? Check with the VA because vets do get a burial allowance around $300 to $700 for non-service related deaths. Check with the VA for full details.
- Donate the body to science. That's a pretty 'far out there' choice for a lot of people. But it does bring the funeral cost to zero. Check with somewhere like Anatomy Gifts Registry for specific details. There may be free cremation services as part of this, with ashes returned to the family in a few weeks.

SUMMARY OF VITAL SERVICES

These are the key points to remember to help a low-income senior have a better quality of life. Please read the more detailed information within the other chapters of this book or do more research online.

1. <u>Doctor Relationship</u>: It is very important that you establish a good rapport with your doctor or the senior's doctor. The doctor will be your strongest ally in obtaining services.
2. A responsible caring person should make sure they have <u>Power of Attorney</u> before the senior's dementia advances to the point where their state of mind can be called into question.
3. In addition to Medicare, make sure they apply for <u>Medicaid</u> as Medicaid pays for an additional host of services that Medicare does not.
4. On a doctor's orders, Medicaid will pay for many pieces of <u>equipment</u> and <u>supplies</u> to be delivered to the senior's home: *portable toilet, shower chair, walker, adult undergarments, bed pads, wheelchair, hospital bed, etc.*
5. <u>Department of Aging: In-Home Support Services</u> – This department can help you find providers who will assist with a variety of duties to help the senior live a safer environment in their home and can provide services outside of the home (*shopping, cooking, cleaning, bathing, help with medications, etc.*) The senior's family member or current caregiver can also be trained and then paid for these services instead of a stranger. The services are "free" to the senior and paid for by the state.

6. <u>Meals on Wheels</u>: Provides hot nutritious meals delivered to the senior's home - free or for a very minimal charge. *No senior should go hungry!*
7. <u>Medicaid Assisted Living Waiver:</u> This program can help the senior qualify for admission to a good quality Assisted Living Facility or Board & Care Facility, and Medicaid will pay the bulk of the fees.
8. <u>Transportation Services:</u> Almost every city and state has either discounts or free transportation services for qualified seniors that will take them and pick them up to and from doctor's appointments, grocery shopping or even trips to the Mall.
9. <u>Hospice:</u> There are some situations where a senior with serious medical conditions can be placed on Hospice even though they are not terminally ill. Consult the doctor, as hospice workers provide a vast array of services coming into your home to help you care for a senior in your charge. The addition of Hospice status "does not" negate your ability to qualify for In-Home Support Services.
10. <u>Caregiver Support Services:</u> Do the research described in earlier chapters to make sure you get respite breaks to relieve the stress of caring for an elderly person.

TERMINOLOGY AND BEYOND

I've added a couple of lines below each term to allow for making notes if you wish. This A-Z listing of terms and services is meant to provide some more information and also give you an easy reference for much of what we've covered in more detail in earlier pages.

Adult Care by the Day (generally called *Adult Day Care*)
These are facilities that provide a place for you to take the senior for a few hours a day, or possibly the whole day. You often have to pay privately for this, but there may be some help with Medicaid. Most will require some coordination with a doctor to sign certain forms so the facility understands any medical conditions the senior faces, medications they take, and the level of watchfulness or care they need to provide. You might find longer term care here for a few days or more.

_____

_____

Adult Protective Services
National Adult Protective Services Agency
www.napsa-now.org
These are the state agencies charged with making sure that seniors are not abused physically, emotionally or financially and that they are getting the help they need if they are being abused. Hospitals, social workers and several other people are mandated by law to report any suspected abuse. But these reports are anonymous and if you know (or strongly suspect) that a senior is being abused, you can and should report it. You can Google

"adult protective services" for your city or county for contact info for your local agency. But please have a fair amount of certainty before reporting as it gets the police, sheriffs and county workers involved. This is not something you should report on a whim. This agency is often part of the Department of Aging Services.

Advance Medical Directive
http://www.caringinfo.org/i4a/pages/index.cfm?pageid=3289

This is a legally recognized form where you designate someone to be in charge of medical decisions on your behalf should you become too ill or mentally impaired to make decisions for yourself. This is not restricted to seniors. Everyone should have a directive; it need not be a relative, just someone you trust will see to your best interest and wishes. Some medical plans or hospitals allow you to keep this on file with them. It is generally best to have it notarized. There are multiple downloadable forms online, including through www.aarp.org

---

Alzheimer's Disease
www.alz.org   AND   www.alzheimers.net
Alzheimer's is a progressive degenerative disorder or disease that gradually worsens over time. There is a gradual loss of memory, changes in behavior, thinking, and language skills.

Alzheimer's is the most common form of dementia and affects upwards of 5 million people a year just in the United States alone. Recall also that Alzheimer's sometimes affects people at a young age, as early as their forties. This is called "early onset Alzheimer's."

If you feel the person for whom you are caring (or another loved one) is exhibiting the signs, it is important that a medical professional provide a formal diagnosis of either dementia or Alzheimer's. This formal diagnosis can lead to more support services through various agencies and medical establishments.

Some agencies provide more general designations for the stages of Alzheimer's, and they may say there is mild, mid-stage and advanced or end-stage.

Dr. Barry Reisberg of New York University (NYU) has developed a ranking of the **7 Stages of Alzheimer's** used by many in the profession, and is summarized below from the alzheimers.net site.

Stage 1: No Impairment
At this stage, some of the changes may not be detectable and there may not be evident memory problems or other symptoms of dementia yet.

Stage 2: Very Mild Decline
The person might exhibit minor memory problems or may lose things around the house, but it looks like normal age-related memory loss.

Stage 3: Mild Decline
They may start to have memory and cognitive problems and not do well on tests. They also may start losing things and have difficulty in the following areas:
- finding the right word during conversations
- remembering names
- planning and organizing

Stage 4: Moderate Decline
- Trouble with simple arithmetic
- May forget their life histories
- Exhibit poor short-term memory (this is evidenced in repeating the same question in a short time)
- Trouble or inability managing finances

Stage 5: Moderately Severe Decline
They may start needing help with many day-to-day activities. Could exhibit:
- Significant confusion
- Can't recall simple details about themselves
- Difficulty dressing appropriately
May still be able to bathe and toilet on their own. Generally, still knows their family members and may remember details about their childhood and youth.

Stage 6: Severe Decline
At this stage, they need constant supervision and frequently require professional care. Symptoms include:
- Confusion of environment and surroundings
- Major personality changes and can have behavior problems
- Need help with activities of daily living such as toileting and bathing

- May only recognize closest friends and relatives
- Loss of bowel and bladder control
- Wandering

Stage 7: Very Severe Decline (Final)
Alzheimer's is a terminal illness, and at this stage patients are nearing death. The person loses the ability to respond to their environment or communicate. They have no insight into their condition and need assistance with all activities of daily living. In the final stages, patients may lose their ability to swallow.

Assisted Living Facility
This term pretty much speaks for itself. It means that the senior might have their own apartment or a shared room with another senior in a facility, but that to some degree or another they need 'assistance' with certain things that will help them live more comfortably (eating, bathing, toileting, dressing, medication). For Medicaid assessment, there is a range of 1-5 in terms of designating the degree of care the senior requires.
(Please also see *Residential Care Facility for the Elderly*)

Board and Care Facility
This is also a live-in facility, state licensed and usually has smaller occupancy (can be as few as six residents).
[Please refer to *Residential Care Facility for the Elderly*]

Caregiver
www.caregiverslibrary.com (national link)
www.inlandcaregivers.com (California Inland Empire)

Literally, this is the person who cares for the senior. There are MANY services available to help alleviate the stress of caregivers and provide general support to help them with the senior's care. Please check with your Department of Aging and/or your medical provider for more information. Kaiser has excellent referral services, as do hospice service agencies. Check out *The Caregiver's Workbook* by Ronald L. Moore, a highly respected book with forms and worksheets. Some agencies also provide assistance for grandparents who are raising their grandchildren.

Community Care Licensing (California)
www.ccld.ca.gov
Every state has some department like this that licenses residential care facilities and other places (like day cares). In California, this division falls under the State Department of Social Services.

Conservatorship
http://www.courts.ca.gov/selfhelp-conservatorship.htm
A conservatorship is a court case where a judge appoints a responsible person or organization (called the "conservator") to care for another adult (called the "conservatee") who cannot care for himself or herself or manage his or her own finances. (courts.ca.gov) - California

You should talk to the self-help desk at the court house or an attorney as to the pros and cons of whether a conservatorship is the best way to go for you and your family. I did everything I needed to in order to handle my father's affairs with Power of Attorney and the advanced medical directive; then becoming the Social Security payee later.

_____

_____

Dementia
Dementia is a condition where the person's brain is deteriorating. It is evidenced mostly by memory loss and a lessened sense of being able to care for one's physical needs; and also a lack of good judgment. Usually doctors will say it is either mild, mid-level or advanced dementia. Alzheimer's is the most advanced form of dementia. But not everyone with dementia advances to Alzheimer's. It is important to have a doctor formally diagnose the patient. If their medical plan has one, refer to a geriatric specialist.

_____

_____

Department of Aging
This is probably the best web link in this book. It gives you the link to every state's senior services or Department of Aging.
http://www.caregiverlist.com/StateInformation.aspx

Every state has its own version of a Department of Aging (and might be called by a slightly different title – like Department of Aging and Elder Services) with a whole host of services that come under that department or agency. Some services include: senior abuse reporting; meals on wheels, transportation services, support groups, and in-home support services.

Disabled
A condition that so impedes you mentally or physically that you are unable to work or severely limited in your ability to work. This qualifies a person for a vast number of services and federal/state benefits.

Durable Power of Attorney (see Power of Attorney)
A Power of Attorney (POA) form is a written legal authorization to represent or act on another's behalf in private affairs, business, and/or some other legal matters. The person authorizing the other to act is the principal, grantor, or donor (of the power). The person given the power is the "attorney in fact" or agent (for the donor). This form is powerful and gives you

(the caregiver) legal authority to handle your loved one's legal (and sometimes medical) affairs. Whether it covers medical issues is a state-by-state issue.

Geriatrics
https://www.americangeriatrics.org/
A medical specialty that deals with the care of the elderly and aging.

HMO – **Health Maintenance Organization**
This is an 'in-network' (meaning you use the HMO doctors, pharmacies, hospital and services that contract with them) for all your care. The general exception is if you have an emergency (like a trip to the ER) when you are somewhere outside of the plan. If you have an HMO, you don't get to just go to a different doctor outside the plan because you want to or prefer them. Kaiser Permanente is one of the largest and best, in my opinion. It is highly rated throughout the nation. It has its own hospitals, clinics, optometrists and multiple other services and specialists, including prescriptions, all within its plan. Dentistry is about the only thing they don't cover.

Hospice Care
National Hospice and Palliative Care Organization
https://www.nhpco.org/
Hospice generally attends to a person's physical and emotional or spiritual needs, providing care for the comfort of chronically ill, terminal or seriously ill patients, helping to alleviate their pain and symptoms. It is generally thought of as "end of life" care. Decades ago, most hospice care was provided for in a separate facility similar to a nursing home or as part of a nursing home. The terminally ill patient would go there to live out the last weeks, months or days of their lives. Today, there are countless hospice agencies that work with families to provide in-home services and skilled care workers who will come to your home to help care for the person. See the chapter on Hospice Care.

In-Home Support Services (IHSS)
These are services provided to low-income seniors that help them have a better quality of life in their own home. These are fantastic services, most totally free to the senior and generally provided through the Department of Aging. YOU, as caregiver, can be paid by the state for providing these services to your parent, loved one or grandparent. Caregivers go through training and a fingerprint screening process. The senior and/or family members can interview various caregivers until you find someone you like. They are paid by the state to come into the senior's home and help them with anything from bathing, shopping, cooking, housecleaning, driving to the doctor's office, etc.

Last Will and Testament

This is a legally binding document that describes how you want your property to be distributed upon your death. Most people feel they need a lawyer to make up a Will. While this is advisable, some folks can't afford a lawyer. Technically, you can make a Will by writing down your wishes on a piece of paper and just signing it. You need to try to make your wishes as clear and comprehensive as possible. And it is worth a few dollars to get it notarized. A notary is not going to review what is in the Will, just verify that you are lucid and can prove you are (with identification) who you say that you are. Just Google "Last Will and Testament" and you will find examples and templates to help you get started. LEGALZOOM has an online process and templates to help you with this for a very reasonable price.

Meals on Wheels

https://www.mealsonwheelsamerica.org/ 888-998-6325
info@mealsonwheelsamerica.org

This is a national program that provides hot meals and light companionship to eligible low-income seniors. There is often a bond that forms by the people delivering the meals and the seniors. There are also volunteer opportunities for you to become one of the people who deliver the meals.

Medicare
www.medicare.gov / 1-800-633-4227
Check the official website for full details. When you work, you pay taxes. And part of the taxes that you pay goes towards Social Security and Medicare. Medicare is health insurance for those 65 and older, as well as the disabled and folks with end-stage renal (kidney) failure.

- Part A is your hospital benefit.
- Medicare Part B covers doctor's visits and some medical equipment. There is a premium for Part B.
- Part C are the health plans offered by a private company that contracts with Medicare *to provide you with all your Part A and Part B benefits.* Medicare Advantage Plans include HMOs (like Kaiser Senior Advantage or Blue Cross). Usually these plans also provide your medications.
- Part D is for prescription drug coverage.

Not everything is covered by "straight" Medicare (Parts A & B); hence, most people have additional supplemental plans in which they enroll to help 'augment' or add to their Medicare benefits (Part C plans). Medicare is not something you get because you are low-income (though you could easily have worked all your life and still qualify for Medicare and Medicaid).

Medicaid / Medi-Cal
www.medicaid.gov/
This is the joint federal-state funded health insurance benefit for low-income individuals. But it is heavily subsidized to the states

by the federal government. Medi-Cal is what Medicaid is called in California. Same program. Medicaid has significant income limitations (check with your local Medicaid office: approximately $935 a month for a single person and $1500 for a couple). It also has limits on the amount of assets (resources) you can have and this varies by state. One can sign up for Medicaid just to get the program to cover your Medicare Part B premiums – QMB (which can be as much as $100 a month). This alone is a good reason to sign up for Medicaid.

Medicaid Assisted Living Waiver (ALW)
This is a government-funded program that helps pay the larger portion of the fees for low-income people to be in a residential care facility. The senior still has to pay a portion of the fees from their own financial resources, retirement and/or Social Security. Generally, the senior is left to keep anywhere from $50 to $150 from their private finances for miscellaneous personal expenditures and the rest goes for the facility fees. Medicaid pays the balance. The senior must be assessed by a nurse or nursing agency to certify that they qualify for placement.

Nursing Home (or Skilled Nursing Home)
Many of us like to call any residential senior living facility this, but there is a major difference between a nursing home and assisted living facility. A nursing home is a facility that provides skilled medical care by nurses, nurse practitioners, doctors and

physical therapists. Placement in a nursing home is done by a doctor and can be done on a temporary or permanent basis. Sometimes a temporary placement in a nursing home can lead to placement in an assisted living facility.

Organ Donor
https://organdonor.gov
There is no age limit to organ donation. The condition of the organs is what is important in this life-giving choice.

Palliative Care
www.getpalliativecare.org
This is a system of referrals and assistance to families and seniors with chronic medical conditions or terminal illnesses that helps with quality of life services, pain management, equipment in the home and support for caregivers.

Power of Attorney (POA) – also see "Durable POA"
This is a legal form (honored in most situations, but not by the Social Security Office) that gives you the legal right to manage / control another person's business, financial affairs and dealings with their personal and (sometimes) real property. Make sure

you use the specific form for your state. This is not a 'federal' form. Each state has its own regulations about the limits and reach of a POA. Get this form signed in front of a notary while the person is still lucid and understands what they are signing.

NOTE: Once again... the U.S. Social Security Office DOES NOT recognize POA in terms of dealing with their office on behalf of someone else. You must become the person's Social Security Payee to deal with SS and Medicaid/Medi-Cal on someone else's behalf. Otherwise, you can speak on their behalf only with the senior present to give authorization.

POLST: Physician Orders for Life-Sustaining Treatment (usually the original is a hot pink form) http://polst.org/

This is a medical form that has a series of questions and boxes that you check to name the person who gets to make decisions for you medically if you are unable to do so (when someone says about 'pulling the plug' this form can designate that). It also gives clear information to the hospital or doctor as to the type of care you wish in terms of "no heroic measures" or if you do or do not want to be on life-sustaining equipment (like a ventilator to help you breath). MOST nursing homes and assisted living facilities insist that this completed form be submitted as part of the admission process and duly signed by the patient and their doctor.

Many states have their own version and many hospitals and HMOs have their own version. It is highly recommended that everyone has one of these, not just the elderly. But it is crucial that you review this and have one for the senior in your care. If you have a regular hospital where the person in your care goes, you should make sure you have a POLST on file with them.

Some states also have what is called "Five Wishes" which does the same thing but is several pages. The POLST is one page and simplifies everything.

_____

_____

Real Property
This is a term that generally refers to land, a house, condo, or other such 'fixed' dwelling. When making a Will, you want to make sure you are clear about your "real property" versus personal effects (like car, clothes, jewelry, and the like).

_____

_____

Rehabilitation Center/Facility (Rehab)
This is an establishment that has trained professionals (generally physical therapists, social workers, possibly psychiatrists) and helps a person heal and become more mobile after an injury or medical trauma like a stroke or broken hip. Some Rehab facilities are non-residential and the person just goes there for treatment and returns home. Most care given at a residential

Rehab Center is geared to restoring the person to good health so they can return home... or to their residential care facility.

_____

_____

Reporting Abuse: This is statewide for care facilities so you will need to look up the reporting agency for your state/county. California Department of Social Services: Community Care Licensing Division Centralized Complaint and Information Bureau; 744 P Street, Sacramento, CA   95814
If you see something, say something – HOTLINE #:
1-844-538-8766

_____

_____

Residential Care Facilities for the Elderly (RCFE)
(ALSO see Assisted Living, Board & Care)

These can be called Assisting Living Facility, Alzheimer's Care Center, Board and Care Facilities and some Retirement Homes. Some states might have a slightly different name for this. Above is the California term. These are **non-medical facilities** that provide a level of **care** that includes assistance with activities of

daily living like bathing, grooming, administering medication and meals. RCFEs in California are licensed by the State Department of Social Services, Community Care Licensing Division. **Medicaid can and does help pay the fees for these facilities nationwide. (see Medicaid Assisted Living Waiver Program in its own chapter.**

Respite Care

Caregivers need a break every now and then from caring for the senior. Respite care is an arrangement that you can set up with an Assisted Living Facility to take your senior into their facility to stay for a few days or a few weeks. This can be quite expensive (maybe $100 or more a day). Depending on what other social services you are receiving, there are sometimes FREE respite services. For instance, if your senior is on Hospice, that agency might provide four or five days of free respite services to the caregiver on a one-time or periodic basis. If the senior has his/her own finances or other family members can chip in, this is a critical break of which to avail yourself.

Senior Citizen

Each state has its own designation, but this is generally categorized as someone over age 62 or 65. Many organizations lower it to age 55. There are a multitude of discounts available to seniors.

Skilled Nursing Home (OR Nursing Home)
Many of us like to call any residential senior living facility this, but there is a major difference between a nursing home and an assisted living facility. A nursing home is a facility that provides skilled medical care by nurses, nurse practitioners, doctors and physical therapists. Placement in a nursing home is done by a doctor and can be on a temporary or permanent basis. Sometimes a temporary placement in a nursing home can transition to admission to an assisted living facility.

Social Services
This term covers a wide range of services by public and private agencies and companies to help older people get the medical, financial and psychological help they need to live their lives in a safe and healthy manner. Many health plans (like Kaiser Permanente) have entire departments set up to help with referral services.

Social Security
http://www.ssa.gov
This is a federal program that provides a monthly income for seniors, starting at age 62. Workers pay into this program via taxes from their paychecks or through self-employment taxes that they pay into the system. If you have enough credits (or payments) into the system, disabled individuals can collect Social Security Disability earlier than age 62. Check with the Social Security office for the most current information, but the age for full retirement benefits is 65 or 66, while some people

wait until age 70 for the most benefits. When you collect earlier (age 62), your benefit is much less and that is a permanent change to your monthly retirement benefit. There are a lot of complicated ins and outs of the Social Security system and you should check directly with that office for detailed information.

_____

_____

Social Security Payee
This is a formal designation that makes a person responsible for receiving a senior's social security income (on the senior's behalf).

_____

_____

Supplemental Security Income (SSI)
This is an additional payment from the Social Security office to people who have very low income. I would approximate under $800 for an individual. But check your state's income and asset limits on the Social Security website. Once a person is receiving SSI, they are automatically eligible for Medicaid.

_____

_____

Will (or Last Will and Testament): This is a document, formal or informal, that gives instructions as to the disposal of your real property, personal belongings and monies after your death.

Generally, you designate an "executor' who will be the person responsible for seeing that the bequeaths in the Will are handled properly. While it is best to have a lawyer handle drawing up a Will, most people with limited resources may not hire a lawyer. There are lots of online forms and packets one can order. But technically a Will can be verbal, written down by hand, or done as a video. It is always best to make sure it is witnessed and that the date and signatures can be verified.

_____

_____

I am almost a hundred years old; waiting for the end, and thinking about the beginning. There are things I need to tell you, but would you listen if I told you how quickly time passes? I know you are unable to imagine this.

Meg Rosoff, *What I Was*

Me and dad (top-1968); bottom 2015

COMPLAINTS and REPORTING

There are several ways that an individual can report known or suspected abuse of a senior by a private individual or a residential care facility. I would only caution that you take such reporting seriously and that your concerns are valid, especially when reporting individuals. Find the appropriate reporting agency for your state.

Adult Protective Services
California
http://www.cdss.ca.gov/inforesources/Adult-Protective-Services

CALL   911

California Department of Aging: Long Term Care Ombudsman   (866) 229-0284

Physical Therapy Board of California
(800) 832-2251

Skilled Nursing Facility: Consumer Complaint
Licensing **http://hfcis.cdph.ca.gov/search.aspx**
The above link has a form you can complete to file complaints.
Complaints   **(SB County)**
(909) 383-4777 or (800) 344-2896

Residential Care Facilities for the Elderly
(includes assisted living, board and care)
(844) 538-8766

REFERENCES

I scoured the Internet and dozens of sites. I give credit to them all. I did not write this book as a journal or scholarly paper. Some references are made within certain sections and some are here. Once again, I am not trying to plagiarize. I gathered a lot of public information and give credit to all. Lots of my own original writing is included here and lots of material from all the other wonderful online resources.
Thank you!

www.medicare.gov
www.ssa.gov
caregiverlist.com/StateInformation.aspx
www.senioradvisor.com/Elderly

CALIFORNIA LINKS

California Inland Empire Care Givers: www.inlandcaregivers.com

Community Care Licensing: www.ccld.ca.gov

California County In-Home Support Services Offices
http://www.cdss.ca.gov/inforesources/County-IHSS-Offices

California Medi-Cal Office
www.dhcs.ca.gov/services/medi-cal

Just remember, when you're over the hill, you begin to pick up speed.

Charles M. Schulz

IN CONCLUSION...

It occurred to me that some people might find some of what I have
written about caring for my father cynical or cold in parts. I hope that
is not the case. I tried to be honest about the fact that this is often an
unpleasant task – caring for the elderly. If one is to undertake it, my
goal was to make sure you understood what a great responsibility it
can be and that it will, quite often, be stressful.

My father was a great influence in my life, despite the fact that as a
child I only lived under the same roof with him for about three years.
Yet he paid for me to go to private school. He took me to my first
Broadway play when I was eight-years old, which led me to a rich life
filled with the arts as the backdrop of my life and as a career. He gave
me the Macy's Thanksgiving Day Parade, ice skating at Rockefeller
Center, and a taste for gourmet food by the time I was nine. His
influence permeated almost every part of the woman I became. And I
like the woman I became.

Yet it does not negate the fact that he was a man with whom I was not
accustomed to living, a man who very much put his own interests and
needs first most of his life. And it made it a very difficult transition
when he came to live with us with his dementia quickly advancing
and his body beginning to break down. Some people age gracefully,
with humor and acceptance of the changes in their life. Dad did not.
And it caused a great deal of friction and stress.

But I took care of him. My husband "Wonderful Rob" took care of
him. I love my father. We gave him a safe, loving place to spend his
last years, and we tried to guard his dignity as much as possible during
the brutal last stages of aging. As Bette Davis once said, "Old age
ain't no place for sissies."

Mostly, what I have learned so far about aging, despite the creakiness of one's bones and cragginess of one's once-silken skin, is this: Do it. By all means, do it.

Maya Angelou

ABOUT THE AUTHOR

Davida Siwisa James was born in Philadelphia, Pennsylvania. She has lived in New York City, Los Angeles, and St. Thomas, U.S. Virgin Islands. Davida has an English degree from UCLA, and she attended the Penn State Dickinson School of Law in Carlisle, Pennsylvania. She is an award-winning short story author (*The Caribbean Writer*), editor, and has written numerous magazine and newspaper articles as a freelance journalist.

She is the managing partner of Fortuna Business Collective, LLC – www.thefortunacollective.com
Davida is also the founder and executive director of Wordsmith Productions, a 501c3 arts nonprofit in California. www.wordsmithproductions.org

Davida's other published titles include:
Imagined Lives (Autobiography; 2014)
The South Africa of His Heart (Memoir; 2007)
Life in Brief (short story-poetry collection)
Just a Note (an epistolary two-act play; 2017)
The Commute; Volume 14 "The Caribbean Writer"
www.davidasiwisajames.com

The author lives in Southern California with her husband, Robelto James and their puppy, Ziggy. Her son, Hudson Obayuwana, is a screenwriter.

123

124

26202399R00078

Made in the USA
San Bernardino, CA
16 February 2019